WARREN BUFFETT AND THE STREET CLEANER

The Secrets Within: A Street Cleaner's Letter to Warren Buffett

by

Jeonghoon, CHOI

CHAPTER 1

•

"Why did you want to meet Mr. Buffett?"

An Uber driver I met in Omaha asked. Strangely, I didn't know the answer to that question. I came all the way to Omaha to meet Mr. Buffett. Still, it was funny that I didn't know why I wanted to meet him. I hoped someone could tell me the answer.

When I was a college student, I suddenly felt the desire to see Warren Buffett, or Mr. Buffett. He had earned a lot of money and was famous for helping many people. Personally, I thought he was an admirable person. If he lived next door to me, I would have liked to give him chocolates as a gift. But he didn't live next door to me. We were complete strangers.

Thus, I set off to Berkshire Hathaway in Omaha. That's where Mr. Buffett worked. I knew that visiting his company wasn't a rational choice to make. But by the time I came to my senses, I was already on a plane to Omaha. Unless I jumped out of the plane, I had no choice but to go to Omaha.

After impulsively arriving at Mr. Buffett's company, I started to ponder a crucial question: how could I actually meet him? I had come to his company without even considering how I would meet him. Simply arriving at his company wasn't the best way to meet him. I needed to come up with a more concrete plan to meet him.

When I first arrived at Mr. Buffett's company, I decided to explore the surroundings. I had come all this way. I wanted to get a better sense of what Mr. Buffett had seen throughout his lifetime.

Mr. Buffett's company stood tall under the burning Omaha sun. I stood there gazing at his building. It stood so beautifully, as if it would guard that spot for decades to come. (To be honest, Mr. Buffett's company looked like an extremely ordinary building. Still, since it was Mr. Buffett's company, I wanted to speak kindly of it.)

After observing Mr. Buffett's company, I took a brief stroll around the area. It was summer at the time, so the weather was sunny and pleasant. Walking along the streets on such a day lifted my spirits.

During my walk, I noticed some litter by the roadside. I picked it up and disposed of it in a trash bin. There weren't any trash bins near Mr. Buffett's company, so I had to use one located a bit further away.

A clean street could surely uplift the mood of those passing by. Suddenly, an idea struck me on how to potentially meet Mr. Buffett: cleaning up around his company. Somehow, I felt that by cleaning, I might have a chance to encounter Mr. Buffett.

Whenever I spotted litter or fallen leaves near Mr. Buffett's company, I swept them away with a broom. I even used a knife to scrape off chewing gum stuck to the ground. Imagining people walking down the street after it had been cleaned and feeling happy made me happy too. Of course, the street was already quite clean even before I started. But I wanted to cherish this space even more. And so, I became the street cleaner around Mr.

Buffett's company.

But I had a strange worry. I found myself becoming afraid of encountering Mr. Buffett. For some reason, as I cleaned around Mr. Buffett's company, the thought of meeting him froze me. Despite it being summer, I could feel a chill as if goosebumps were rising on my skin. It felt like watching a horror movie alone in a vast theater. I couldn't understand why I was so afraid of meeting Mr. Buffett. Could it be that Mr. Buffett was a ghost?

I had come to Omaha to meet Mr. Buffett. However, now I almost believed I no longer wanted to meet him myself. Still, I continued to go to Mr. Buffett's company and clean around it. Then, in a conversation with an Uber driver, I came to understand why I was afraid to meet Mr. Buffett.

I had used Uber once to go to a mart in Omaha to buy some groceries. The Uber driver who picked me up was very outgoing. As we rode together, he told me about some great sights in Omaha. I told him that I had come to Omaha because I wanted to meet Mr. Buffett. After hearing my story, he asked me, "Why did you want to meet Mr. Buffett?" It was then that I realized I didn't know why I wanted to meet Mr. Buffett after all.

I realized why I was afraid to meet Mr. Buffett. The reason was that I didn't know why I wanted to meet him in the first place. I felt like I wouldn't be able to say anything if I had met Mr. Buffett and he asked me, "Why did you come to see me?" I was afraid of being speechless in front of Mr. Buffett.

I couldn't figure out why I wanted to meet Mr. Buffett. I pondered deeply, but I couldn't find the answer. Perhaps I went to meet him because I wanted to know the answer itself.

Many people were curious about why I went to meet Mr. Buffett. Some wondered if I was interested in stock investing. Others wondered if I wanted to make a lot of money. Since Mr. Buffett was known for making a fortune through stock investing, they asked such questions.

However, personally, I didn't aspire to invest in stocks or make a lot of money. Of course, there were times when I felt I wanted to be like Mr. Buffett. Still, for me, he was like Santa Claus. Santa Claus was someone who could give gifts to all the children in the world. But when we thought of Santa Claus, we didn't think of his warehouses full of gifts or bank accounts full of money to buy all the gifts. Instead, we thought of Christmas. Santa Claus was the one who could gift Christmas to children. So, I saw Mr. Buffett as Santa Claus. He was someone who showed me a world I had not seen before.

I was curious about why I recognized Mr. Buffett as a special figure. Whenever I saw him on media, I couldn't help but feel that he was different from me. But I couldn't figure out why he was different. Where did his uniqueness come from? Was it his white hair? Some say power sometimes comes from the hair, according to the Bible. Would I become special too if I had white hair like Mr. Buffett when I got older?

Of course, everyone knew that age or hair couldn't bring about uniqueness. Even I, who once forgot to submit my exam paper after completing all the questions and went home, knew that fact. Fortunately, there was a moment when I found a clue to understand his secret. There was a moment when I felt the same sense of specialness within myself that I once felt from Mr. Buffett. It happened when I did something that I usually didn't do.

I've had ADHD, Attention Deficit/Hyperactivity Disorder, a condition with emotional anxiety, since I was young. For someone with ADHD, it's like sitting in a room with dozens of noisy TVs. That's why focusing on something could be difficult for me. Imagine different televisions playing 'The Matrix' and 'The Lion King' in front of someone. How could he possibly focus on what he was doing? If there was someone who could focus on his work despite those movies playing on the TVs, I'd give him a dollar. (No, a dollar is a bit much. How about 25 cents?)

Personally, I didn't want to reveal my shameful side to others. It was like underwear. I always kept it with me, but I never showed it. That was why I didn't like to tell others about my ADHD condition. It was a weakness, and weakness was shameful. Unless I was a superman who wore underwear above his pants, I didn't have to show how dirty my underwear was.

However, there was a moment when my college friend shared his secret with me. In that moment, I had to share mine with him as well.

I attended college in the United States. The university was truly filled with students from various countries. Looking at our university, which was a gathering of diverse races, felt like looking at a small universe.

Our university had numerous student communities. There was a community made up of students from my home country, South Korea. There were also student communities like drinking groups or soccer clubs. There were so many student communities at our university that I couldn't even know all the different types.

One of the student communities I joined was the international student group. It was a community that welcomed all international students. People in the group and I would sometimes go bowling at the bowling alley on campus. There were also movie theaters and restaurants near the school, so we would occasionally go out to watch movies or have meals together.

Even though I wasn't an outgoing person, I liked to spend time within the group. In that community, I met a friend who was of a different race from me. He wasn't particularly noticeable in the group. Like me, he was also a quiet person. He was kind and didn't refuse when others asked for help. Sometimes, even when I asked for help with assignments, he would assist me. Our university was known for its heavy workload, so he must have been busy with his own assignments. Yet he always helped others without hesitation. However, after fulfilling someone's request, he never opened up again.

One day, when we were deciding on a lunch menu in our group, we started discussing what we wanted to eat as usual. I used to enjoy the cafeteria food when I was at university. There were places on campus that served pizza or hamburgers. However, I didn't want to eat on campus with this group of friends. It wasn't very common for us to gather. I wanted to make our time together as special as possible. Many of the other friends shared a similar sentiment, and because of us, we often ended up having meals outside of campus.

On that day, we decided to go eat outside. We were all excited. However, I realized something about my friend who often helped others but remained silent: he never mentioned his favorite menu. I had never seen him showing his own preference for the food. When people decided on a menu, he would simply follow us without saying a word.

Thus, I asked him without much thought, "What kind of food do you like?"

It was a question without much significance. I simply asked him the same question I would ask anyone else. However, for some reason, it seemed to hold great meaning for him.

A few days later, as we coincidentally crossed paths and walked together, we didn't exchange many words. We weren't particularly close, so I didn't feel the need to strike up a conversation, especially as I was heading to another class. I often felt exhausted during classes, so I couldn't invest much energy in socializing between the classes.

But then he suddenly said, "Thank you for asking me what I wanted to eat back then."

At first, I didn't quite understand what that meant. I hadn't really done anything to warrant his gratitude before. But then it hit me that the only recent interaction we had was when I asked him about the menu.

"It's no big deal," I said to him with a sincere tone. I didn't think asking him about his favorite menu was anything remarkable. However, he seemed genuinely thankful, so I responded to his gratitude with a more serious demeanor.

We became much closer. I wasn't someone who talked a lot when I was with others. However, he understood my disposition. He didn't mind if I didn't say anything and just played with my phone while we were together. He would respond when I initiated conversation, and if I was occupied with my own tasks, he did his own thing too.

One day, like always, he and I were studying together at the library until late. Our school dormitory had good desks for studying, but since the dorm was also a resting space, it was hard to concentrate on studying there. So, I often went to the library with friends to study.

The library was about a 20-minute walk from the dormitory. It was nicely organized, and studying there always made me feel smarter for some reason. Of course, I realized it was just a feeling of illusion every time I took an exam.

On the way from the dormitory to the library, there was a large playground. Our university didn't have a soccer stadium, but instead, there was a large artificial turf field. Students would bring their own small goalposts and play soccer or baseball there. I usually enjoyed playing soccer. Ever since I learned soccer from a senior I admired during high school, soccer had become my favorite sport.

My friend and I stopped by the stadium on our way back from the library. It was late, so there was nobody at the stadium. All the lights at the stadium went off after 10 PM, leaving only silence in the air.

I usually didn't want to go straight home when studying late into the evening. No matter how tired I was, I wanted to take a break, even if just for a little while. The best relaxation was a good night's sleep. However, relying solely on sleep to relieve fatigue seemed to diminish the interest in life. So, even if I didn't have much time to rest during the day, I would take short breaks even if it meant reducing my sleep time.

Taking breaks wasn't anything special. Sometimes I'd lie on my bed and use my phone, and other times I'd go for a walk. On that particular day, I decided to sit down with my quiet friend at the field and have a chat.

The conversation with my friend was enjoyable. We didn't delve into anything profound or crack jokes. Instead, we simply asked each other about things we hadn't known before. I asked him about his home country, and he asked me about mine.

Then, I suddenly became curious about why he came to study abroad. So, I asked him about the reasons behind his decision to study abroad. However, he calmly shared a shocking story.

"I ran away to the United States because I was raped by my father. I became gay because I was raped so often." He spoke in such a matter-of-fact tone. Yet, in that moment, I felt my skin stiffen like reptilian scales. I wanted to confirm if I had understood his words correctly. However, through his voice, I realized I had. His tone was composed, yet it carried a profound sadness.

I had become quite close with him. Until then, he didn't seem to carry any problems. However, when I heard his story, I realized the pain he couldn't express. He was someone with a secret that was difficult to share with others. Yet, somehow, he confided in me. Why did he tell me his secrets? What did he want from me?

I glanced at him for a moment, and strangely, he showed no expression at all. Instead, he seemed to gaze calmly at the sky. His expression remained the same as always. It was as if he had lived without any problems. However, his eyes, as he looked at the sky, seemed so lonely.

In that moment, I didn't feel like ignoring his story. His secret was a sensitive issue for him, but I wanted to say something, anything. What could I say to him that would be helpful? I couldn't come up with a clear answer. Usually, I would offer comfort to a friend going through a hard time. But at the stadium, I couldn't offer comfort to my friend. His secret seemed like something that couldn't be comforted by any words.

As we sat there in silence, my friend gazing at the sky while I focused on the stadium in front of me, it felt like we might just stay there quietly and go home separately. My friend didn't seem to expect me to say anything. If I left without a word, he probably wouldn't blame me. But I didn't want to just let him go. If I sent him home like that, he might feel like there was no one who understood his struggles. So, after gathering my thoughts for a moment, I began to speak to him.

"Did I tell you that I've struggled with ADHD and have been to a psychiatric hospital before?" My friend looked at me with a surprised expression for a moment. "No, this is the first time I'm hearing about it," he replied.

Without looking at his face, I continued calmly, "I've struggled with severe anxiety since I was young. So, I've experienced a lot of bullying from others. But now, it's gotten a lot better. Except for when it gets really bad and it's hard to breathe or my chest hurts, I'm doing much better."

I had never told anyone about my experience with ADHD. I didn't plan on telling anyone in the future either. That story only left painful memories for me. However, after learning that my friend had a difficult secret, I chose to tell him mine.

I finished speaking and silently looked out at the stadium. The stadium still echoed with nothing but silence. I could sense my friend growing quieter. He was once again gazing at the sky. Somehow, he seemed to wear a slightly more serene expression. In the dimness of the stadium, I hadn't really seen him properly, but why did it feel that way?

We stayed silent for a while. Then, I asked him, "Shall we head home now?" He nodded in agreement and we both got up from our seats.

After that conversation, we continued to be friends as before. It felt like nothing had really changed before and after that conversation. We still went to the library together when we wanted to study, and sometimes we walked home together. However, I felt more comfortable spending time with him for some reason. He didn't show it, but it seemed like he regarded me a bit more specially.

I didn't know why I wanted to take the risk of sharing my secret. It wasn't my obligation to empathize with someone's pain. I could just ignore his story.

I used to believe that sharing painful secrets with others was meaningless. Not many people really cared about the other's pain. However, when I heard my friend's story, he felt so lonely.

He looked like a man who had no space for himself. He was a man raped by his own father. Even his home wasn't a place for him.

Thus, I thought he needed some space for himself. I decided to be the one for him. People need some time and space when they pass through hard times. I believe I wanted to become a man who could provide them in the future.

For me, Mr. Buffett was the one who could do so. That's why I wanted to become someone like him. I guess I embarked on a journey to Omaha because I wanted to see with my own eyes the image of who I wanted to become.

CHAPTER 2

• •

I didn't live a life worthy of applause. Instead, I lived a life closer to an ordinary extra fading into the background without even a line in the movie. The only consolation to me was that I didn't live a life like a villain tormenting someone. I was just someone who would live unnoticed and disappear unnoticed.

Still, I didn't view my life too pessimistically. I personally believed that a quiet life was also a meaningful one. Even a painful life could be meaningful at times. At times, bad things could happen in my life. Especially in my past, sad events occurred frequently. However, even when such things happened, I didn't lose much spirit. Just because sad things happened didn't mean I had to live a sad life. Similarly, just because bad things happened didn't mean I had to keep them as bad memories.

Fortunately, at least in my case, the nature of memories aligned with my values most of the time. Except for some cases, the memories have a unique tendency to become glorified over time. Even painful memories would gradually heal with the passage of time. So when heartbreaking events occurred, I trusted that time heals all wounds and waited until my painful memories no longer hurt. In most cases, memories were indeed a source of gratitude.

Still, there were moments when memory became quite stubborn and didn't get along well with my mind. That's why memories I shouldn't forget tend to go missing from my head sometimes. For example, when I tried to remember what I needed to buy at the convenience store, it just didn't come to mind.

On the other hand, memories I sometimes want to forget never seem to disappear. For example, trauma is like that. I experienced a lot of bullying from a young age. There was a time in elementary school when a classmate discovered my ADHD symptoms. That friend told all the students in the class about my symptoms. As a result, I was labeled as mentally ill in the class. That memory, unlike others, wasn't glorified for me. I actively tried to forget that memory. Unfortunately, though, I vividly remember even the nuances of the voices the kids used back then.

No one wants to remember situations where they didn't feel loved in detail. However, no one could completely forget such memories. Everyone just pretends as if those things never happened.

But I tended to live positively. When I had experiences like trauma, I laughed it off, saying, "Trauma is like first love." First love was actually a memory I didn't want to remember like trauma, but I couldn't forget it.

When I was in college, I met my first love. However, my first love transferred to another school, and I strongly wished to forget her. However, she dared to appear in my dreams, always offering a sweet smile. Even without kissing her lips, I could taste the sweetness of the smile. I still wonder why she showed a smile that I couldn't see in the real world.

I used to ponder why first love was so painful. When I think about it, my first love wasn't the most beautiful girl in the world. Of course, she was beautiful. I heard rumors that she attended church, so I started going to the same church every week. A pastor at the church believed that he had met a devout believer, because I went to the church every week. He once asked me why I came to the church every week. I couldn't admit that I was going to church because of a girl. I claimed that I came to church every week because I met Jesus. The pastor was quite happy. I was glad that he was happy. Still, although I wasn't a devout Christian, I felt guilty for lying in church. However, I heard that merciful Jesus forgives all sins. It would have been nice if he could forgive me for my lie too.

Anyway, my first love was certainly the most memorable person from my past. Why did I remember her so vividly? Now that I think about it, the reason I couldn't forget my first love wasn't because she was beautiful or cute. It was simply because that love never came true. There are things that become so beautiful precisely because I can't have them.

Trauma was similar in that regard. The difficulty of trauma didn't come from the pain itself, but rather from the inability to have the life I wanted at that time. Ultimately, trauma was like first love. So, while I couldn't necessarily forget trauma like I couldn't forget first love, I didn't have to deliberately dwell on it. Personally, I didn't want to keep recalling painful memories. Living by laughing off even the painful memories was a healthy way of life. I didn't feel the need to tell anyone about these painful memories, nor did I feel the need for anyone to hear them. Whenever I shared these painful memories with others, they hurt me, and they were tired of listening.

Still, I wanted to write down the stories of old traumas in this book. It was because, through these memories, I came to understand why I wanted to meet Mr. Buffett.

I moved a lot from a young age because my father had a job that required frequent transfers. Every time my father received a new assignment in a different area, I had to move, and I had to transfer to a new school.

The reason I finally settled down was because my father changed his job. His previous occupations involved frequent transfers. However, my father decided to stay at one job for a long time. As a result, I was able to attend the same school for a longer period, starting from middle school.

However, there were also problems at the new school. Because I moved schools so frequently, I didn't have the chance to develop social skills. Every time I changed schools, I had to make new friends all over again. Just when I started to get to know someone, it was time to move again. As a result, I wasn't really good at making friends.

And so, before I knew it, I was in middle school. Because I didn't develop many social skills before, I couldn't make many friends. Moreover, due to my ADHD condition, many people recognized me as a troublemaker rather than their potential friend.

The problem happened when the bullies tried to harass me. They knew that I didn't have many friends to ask for help. Thus, the bullies who disliked me would call me out and often beat me up. They were quite intimidating.

Most kids at the school were going through puberty as they entered middle school, which led to the appearance of some really large students. A few had grown incredibly tall and strong. They seemed like they could win a fight against an adult. So, I had to be cautious not to provoke them unnecessarily. I couldn't afford to engage in a fight, as I'd likely get beaten up.

Unfortunately, sometimes, no matter how careful I was, problems would inevitably arise. The kids who had grown strong and tall began to show off their strength. I was, sometimes, unaware and would do things that would earn their ire. Eventually, their tormenting became a daily occurrence for me.

I had no intention of resisting the bullies. Honestly, resisting them caused more pain. They liked to hurt more when the victims resisted. Thus, the best way to avoid any harm from the bullies was to act like a fool. They laughed at a fool instead of hurting him. Thus, I dared to act like a clown in front of them.

My school life wasn't fun. As a student, I was asked to be a good student at the school. Still, the school was like a book with no charm that even the author wouldn't want to read. However, fortunately, a twist came into my life. It turned out that I didn't know much about the world. There were new worlds that I had never known before. I realized the simple fact when I found a torn comic book I stumbled upon in a park.

It was one of those days when I was daydreaming while strolling through the park. I didn't like to be in a place with a large population and noise. I liked to think of strange topics without intervention. Imagining the world that I hadn't seen was my hobby.

Fortunately, on that day, there were a few people around. I decided to take a leisurely walk. I could look for a space to sit down and spend time imagining. Still, I chose to take a walk. When I stayed in one place alone for a long time, people would often stare at me. I didn't like to earn people's interest. Moreover, walking somehow stimulated new imagination. Thus, I liked to walk while imagining.

The ground felt damp, perhaps from a recent drizzle. The air was still a bit moist. It was pleasantly cool. Just breathing in the fresh air seemed to alleviate stress. On beautiful days, even just taking a breath could become a pill for pain.

Then, I found myself sitting on a bench. Walking had become tiring, so I occasionally rested before heading back home. On that particular day, while sitting on the bench, I noticed a nearly torn-apart book next to a trash bin. It was a type of book I hadn't seen before. It appeared to have been exposed to the rain, with blotches and significant tears. It looked like the face of someone who had indulged in too much alcohol and spent the night vomiting.

The book was a comic book. I approached it cautiously, as it was in poor condition and seemed ready to fall apart at the slightest touch. It felt like something I might tear apart with my bare hands at a carnival.

The cover had a sticker with the address of a certain comic book store.

"Dayoung Comic Book Café."

Beneath the address, there was another phrase:

"Daehi Stationery Store, 2nd floor."

It was a description of the location of the Comic Book Café. I was quite familiar with that stationery store as I frequented it often. It was conveniently located near my school. I would often go there to buy school supplies. Surprisingly, it never seemed to run out of any school supplies, despite serving numerous students. How could they always have everything in stock? It was like Santa's gift box where anything I wished for magically appeared. (Still, it wasn't Santa's. I had to pay to buy things in the stationery store.)

After checking the sticker, I carefully opened the torn comic book. I didn't want to damage it further. I started reading the first few pages. Surprisingly, I found myself entering a new world.

The comic book I had found told the story of a young man searching for a wicked doll. This wicked doll had no heart and tormented people. The protagonist of the comic confronted and destroyed the dolls that hindered his journey. However, even the mighty protagonist couldn't save any of his comrades. The dolls were incredibly strong. One by one, his friends met their demise. In the end, the protagonist had to watch helplessly as his friends were all killed.

The comic book was truly shocking. Every aspect of it was negative. It was a story I had never encountered before. In the stories of movies or novels I had known, good things always happened to the protagonists. They could overcome any kind of obstacles. However, the protagonist of the comic I found in the park was unable to experience anything but despair. He couldn't do anything while his friends were dying. He lost his limbs, becoming like a heartless doll himself. It was a story of unforgettable failure.

I always thought that stories in the world should be filled with happy moments. Even sad stories were meant to pave the way for a happier ending. However, the author of the comic book showed no mercy for his characters. Perhaps the author was one of the heartless dolls in his comic.

Interestingly, despite its overwhelming despair, it forced me to watch the protagonist struggle in vain. I found myself strangely captivated. Even though the ending was so sorrowful, the sadness I felt at that moment had a charm that was beyond expression.

I couldn't understand how a comic book had captivated me like that. I thought books, including comics, had no connection with me. I had never been so drawn to a book before. I thought books only talked about materials that I had to learn. But this comic book was different. This comic book was purely for entertainment. It didn't depict the history of a dynasty, nor did it contain cliché scientific explanations. It was just a tool for the author to depict the world he had imagined.

I used to think that books were meant to impart valuable life lessons to the reader. However, perhaps true books were meant to be a tool for expressing the new world.

People used to tell me that reading books could help people to develop insight. But I didn't like to read books when I was young, which was a concern for my parents. Eventually, my parents realized that I absolutely refused to read books with written text. In the end, my parents bought me comic books, hoping that I would at least read something, even if it was in the form of comics.

Comic books were popular among children. Since I disliked books with written text, my parents hoped I would read comics instead. However, the comic books that my parents bought were different from the one that I found in the park. They were all covered with textbook-like content.

One of the comic books that my parents bought was 'Distant Neighbor,' a comic book that portrayed history in a graphical format. I really disliked memorizing all the events in history. I refused to learn it. Memorizing what happened in the past was none of my concern. That's why my parents bought me 'Distant Neighbor.' They hoped that I could enjoy history by reading a comic book. However, I ignored them all. After reading the first few pages, I realized that the book wasn't the one I was looking for.

The only comic book that I found somewhat interesting among the ones that my parents bought was a comic book about the Bible. My parents even bought me comic books related to the Bible to teach me its contents.

The comic book about the Bible was much more interesting than other comics about history or math. To be honest, comics like 'Distant Neighbor' were no different from history textbooks. Well, at least they were in comic format, which made it somewhat helpful for someone like me. However, the content was still full of facts and names that needed to be memorized for exams, making me uninterested.

In that sense, the comic book about the Bible was much more engaging. It had diverse portrayals of people's emotions and conflicts. The Bible itself was written in a way that was quite engaging for readers.

But the comic book I found in the park was way more exciting than any book I had ever read. Up until then, I felt that other comic books I had read tried to make uninteresting subjects seem fun. Even the Bible comic book seemed more like a tool for delivering Bible stories than pure entertainment. So, I didn't consider comic books as an interesting genre before I had met the torn comic book in the park.

Reading the comic book I found in the park was like tasting candy for the first time. When a child tastes candy for the first time, his eyes should light up. When I tasted candy for the first time in the hospital, I could almost forget the fear I had just experienced with the dentist. The shock of that comic book I found in the park was comparable to that memory.

When I found the comic book in the park, I devoured the entire content in an instant. Time passed quickly. I spent too much time reading it. I knew I would get scolded by my mother for coming home late. But I wanted to read it again. So, I read it once more until late at night, knowing I would face my grandmother's angry daughter.

Before going home, I left the comic book where I first found it, next to the trash can. I thought if someone lost it, he might come back to find it. It could have been discarded, but I wanted to give the owner a chance to reclaim it. (Thinking back now, I think it would have been better for me to return the book to the Comic Book Café. I guess I wasn't so clever when I was young.)

I wanted to read that comic book again if possible. Fortunately, I didn't need to go back to the trash can to find it. I had memorized the location of the Comic Book Café that was written in the comic I found.

'Daehi Stationery Store, 2nd Floor.'

I wrote it down in a small note to remember. Now, all I had to do was visit that place the next day.

I later found out that the Comic Book Café was called a "manhwa-bang." I didn't know at the time, but it seemed to be quite famous.

As soon as school ended, I headed straight to the Comic Book Café. It was located on the upper floor of the stationery store I often visited. It was right in front of the school. I passed by the stationery store and went up the stairs, looking around. Then, I spotted a sign.

'Dayoung Comic Book Café.'

It was the place I had been searching for.

When I entered the Comic Book Café, one thing immediately caught my eye. The cafe was covered in pictures of comic book characters, all over the walls. Some of the pictures were so large that it seemed like I could lie down and sleep on them, although they were probably too thin and would tear easily.

I took a moment to look at the posters hanging on the walls. Most of them featured various comic book characters, each with different expressions. Some characters had expressions that no human could possibly make. In some pictures, the characters' mouths were stretched wider than their foreheads. I couldn't recall ever seeing such expressions even in movies. It seemed like comic books were a genre that freely incorporated such unrealistic expressions. Otherwise, I would have to say that the author of the comic book wasn't aware of the structure of human skeleton and muscle.

I wondered how the comic book artist came up with such expressions. Perhaps comic books allowed us to depict the expressions we wanted to make but couldn't in real life.

I approached the door of the Comic Book Café. When I opened it, I heard a small bell ringing. I glanced up and noticed a small bell hanging above the door. It was an alarm bell to alert the owner when a customer entered. The bell's soft chime signaled my arrival. It did its job well.

A voice inside the Comic Book Café greeted me. It was none other than the owner of the Comic Book Café. The owner was a middle-aged woman who appeared to be around my parents' age. She might have had children of her own; I had a feeling she did. The way she looked at me, with warmth and care, was like how a mother would look at her child. It was as if she treated me not as a customer but as a family member. If she didn't have a family, I could hardly expect her to give such a look.

I nodded politely in response to her greeting. It was a matter of respect to greet adults properly. I made a conscious effort to maintain that attitude. I reminded myself to always be courteous, especially to those who left a good impression on me. The owner quickly picked up on my lack of knowledge about how things worked there. The comic books were displayed on shelves. Customers could pick out the ones they wanted to read. All I had to do was to choose a comic book, bring it to the owner, and pay a small fee to read it. If I returned the book by the due date, that was all there was to it.

However, being new to the Comic Book Café, I was unaware of this system. So, all I could do was wander around aimlessly, not knowing what to do.

The owner, who was quite perceptive, approached me and asked if it was my first time. I nodded, and she kindly explained how things worked. She suggested a comic book for me to read and mentioned that I could borrow it. It cost about 30 cents for one book, a reasonable amount. If I wanted to purchase a comic book instead of borrowing it, it would cost around $7, which was too expensive for me. Reading comic books without spending too much was a way for me to enjoy them.

I decided to borrow a comic book for the first time. I chose the one recommended by the owner and borrowed it. That single book marked the beginning of my new hobby.

Reading comic books was fabulous. Since then, visiting Comic Book Café and borrowing a comic book became part of my daily routine. I started going to the Comic Book Café right after school from the next day onwards. There, I would borrow 1 or 2 comic books and read them.

Usually, after school, I didn't go straight home. I had another place to go to before heading home. That was my private tutoring institute, also known as a hagwon. It was a separate institution for additional study. I could stop by home before going to the hagwon, but I didn't have much time to relax. The hagwon classes started shortly after school ended. So, I usually took a short break and then went straight to the hagwon after school.

Initially, I didn't have a designated place to relax before going to the hagwon. I wanted to look for a place that had air conditioning, especially during hot summer days, where I could take some rest. Any place without mosquitoes but with air conditioning was what I was looking for. However, it wasn't easy to find such a place.

Fortunately, I found one, finally. The perfect place for all these requirements turned out to be the Comic Book Café. It always had air conditioning. There were no mosquitoes. So, I often spent my time there until my hagwon classes started.

During my time in Korea, I attended hagwon every day, even on Saturdays. Sundays were the only days without classes, but I was given homework to complete at home. It seemed like the teachers were unaware that weekends were meant to be holidays. I wished they could understand that.

Many students, overwhelmed by the intense study at hagwon, ended up dozing off in regular school classes. Despite not being the most diligent student at hagwon, I still wondered why I ended up dozing off in school.

Despite the challenges, there was a reason most students attended hagwon. Some hagwon teachers were truly exceptional, known as "jokjipgae," which roughly translates to "experts at picking topics." These teachers had an amazing ability to select the exact content that would appear in exams and teach it to the students. Under the guidance of such teachers, it was almost impossible for grades not to improve. They improved my grades as well, despite my aversion to studying hard. My hagwon teacher must have been an incredible "jokjipgae."

Going to school and then the hagwon afterward was exhausting. I was constantly tired. At that time, I didn't have any room for activities like games or even healthy outdoor activities like sports. I was buried in academics every day. Thus, the Comic Book Café was indeed a special place for me. It provided me with the only brief moment of relaxation in my daily routine.

Unfortunately, there were moments when the relaxation in the Comic Book Café was not enough to relieve my stress. Sometimes, I was too stressed by my life in school. My life in school was even tougher than that in hagwon.

School and hagwon were quite different for me. At hagwon, I could quit anytime I wanted. I was a customer. No one could blame me for quitting. So, if there were people bothering me at the current hagwon, I could switch to a different one. In contrast, quitting school whenever I wanted wasn't allowed. It wasn't easy to change schools without acceptable reasons. Thus, even when I was in the same class with terrible bullies, I had to adapt to my life in it. However, it wasn't easy for me.

Around the bullies, I had to handle the situation carefully to avoid provoking them. I didn't confront them directly. Instead, I tried to do what they asked me to do. If they wanted me to act like a fool, I became a fool. They would often stop bothering me if I did as they instructed and enjoyed it to some extent. Still, there were times when I got into trouble, even when I tried my best to please them. In such cases, all I could do was to wish to avoid extreme harassment.

Nevertheless, there were some moments when I somewhat enjoyed this foolish routine. Not all bullies were terrible people after all. Some even shared cake with me on their birthdays. It felt quite strange because I had never been invited to a birthday party before.

Still, life with the bullies was like walking on a knife's edge. I didn't know when I was going to be cut. I had to be extremely careful.

I generally avoided getting into major trouble with the bullies at school. If I sensed trouble brewing, I would steer clear of it. There was a consequence for doing what they didn't like.

A good example was my fellow friend, whom I called Maple Story friend. In my class, there were a few others who were also bullied. Bullies liked to have a feast with more than one prey.

Maple Story friend was also a prey of the bullies. He was quite chubby, just like me. He used to be friends with me, but at some point, he distanced himself from me. He started hanging out with the bullies and began behaving like them.

The friend had a strong sense of pride. He didn't want to appear weak in front of others. Occasionally, he aspired to be like the bullies, acting as if their taunts didn't bother him. I generally lowered my pride and acted like a fool to avoid trouble with bullies. In contrast, he wanted to show the bullies that he could be just as strong as them. However, I knew that he wasn't as daring as he wished to appear.

I personally thought he was putting on a bit of a show. I could understand why he did so. Nobody wanted to appear weak or be humiliated. He tried to act indifferent when the bullies taunted him. He wanted to show his daring spirit in front of the bullies. However, he didn't have the courage to fight back. Thus, whenever the bullies hit him, he pretended that he didn't care about bullies harassing him.

The bullies usually didn't pay much attention to my friend as long as he didn't challenge them directly. However, when he displayed signs of not liking their taunts, it became problematic. He acted quite arrogantly at times. When he did that, I could sense that the bullies were uncomfortable. They didn't want someone they bullied to act like one of them, but Maple Story friend didn't seem to pick up on their discomfort.

Maple Story friend, who was harassed by the bullies, was a big fan of games, just like me. Our lives seemed quite similar. Nowadays, after work, I spend my time either playing games or sleeping at home.

In South Korea, there was a famous game called "Maple Story." Maple Story friend was a skilled player in Maple Story. Because of that, I used to call him my Maple Story friend.

He would often share new information about the game with me. He was almost a professor of the game. Since he liked to talk about the game all the time, he didn't hesitate to spend time with others talking about it.

One day, the bullies showed some interest in the game. They asked Maple Story friend how the game was. When the bullies showed interest in Maple Story, he enthusiastically shared information about the game with them. He especially focused on teaching them the basics, as they were new players. He was eager to help them.

Maple Story friend was dreaming of playing games with the bullies and truly becoming friends with them. He was determined to bring them into the game. He was ready to offer any help they needed, even showing a strong sense of responsibility. Maple Story friend was thrilled by the idea that the bullies might need him.

"We can be a great team together!" he said with a hopeful smile.

His enthusiasm was contagious. At first, I thought Maple Story friend being too excited could endanger him. The bullies didn't like to see someone in a good mood, especially when he's not one of them. Still, I started to feel less uneasy about the situation. I thought that they could actually become friends. And it didn't take long to realize that I was wrong.

A few days later, I overheard a conversation between the bullies and my friend.

"Hey, I deleted the account you told me about."

One of the bullies said it briefly. Initially, I didn't fully understand, but it turned out that Maple Story friend had given them his game account details. Maple Story was quite a challenging game for beginners. The more time I invested, the stronger my character became, and the more enjoyable the game became. The bullies asked Maple Story friend to share his game account and password with them. They wanted to use his character together.

Maple Story friend's account was something he had built over several years. Normally, people should never share their personal information like that. However, Maple Story friend wanted to introduce the bullies to the joy of the game so much that he shared his account information with them. He believed that his strong character could stimulate the bullies to spend more time on the game. After all, friends share the most precious things with each other.

But Maple Story friend didn't realize that true friends didn't ask for personal information. The only reason that the bullies wanted to know his account and password was to remove something that he liked. The bullies wanted to make sure that he was only a prey. Because Maple Story friend wanted to pretend like he was one of the bullies, they made him recognize his rank. In the end, Maple Story friend lost his account. The bullies knew how to hurt their prey. They were truly the predators.

Once deleted, he couldn't recover a game account. It was like a person who had passed away and couldn't come back. In the game world, characters could die and come back, but if an account was deleted, the characters had nowhere to return to. I wondered what expression Maple Story friend's in-game character would have. Game characters didn't have emotions, but I imagined that it would have a similar expression to Maple Story friend at that moment—lost and without a place to go. He lost his character and his friends. Of course, the bullies weren't his friends, but he thought they were.

The bullies were glad to see his sadness. Usually, when they were annoyed, they harassed weak people, like Maple Story friend, physically. However, when they saw him feeling harshly depressed after they deleted his account, they tried to console him hypocritically. Lack of physical harassment made Maple Story friend even more miserable.

After witnessing that, I never shared my true feelings with the bullies again. I was already cautious around them, but that incident made me even more careful. I was afraid of them. I felt like they would use even my honest emotions against me.

Comic Book Café was a place where I could escape from the bullies and the pressures of school. The bullies didn't have any interest in comic books. Thus, it was a safe place.

I never revealed to the bullies that I enjoyed reading comic books. I didn't want to give them any more information about me. The less they knew about me, the better our relationship, or lack thereof, would be. Personally, I didn't want to become friends with them or share any laughs with them.

I tried to avoid running into the bullies after school. In fact, I was even more afraid of encountering them after school than during school hours. I feared that if I ran into them after school, I might face harassment outside of school grounds. The area outside of school could be even more dangerous than inside. Inside the school, there were at least other students around, so there were witnesses to their actions. In contrast, imagine encountering them where there were no witnesses, like an empty playground or a park. It could have been a truly terrifying experience. Violence became harsher when there were no restrictions.

I tried my best to avoid meeting the bullies after school. Still, even my efforts weren't enough to save my day. One day, I had to wait outside the hagwon until it opened, and one of the bullies saw me. He told the other bullies that I went to the hagwon after school. From that day on, the bullies would wait for me outside the hagwon every time my class ended, and they would harass me. They hit me whenever they met me. They hit quite hard, and it was painful every time.

That's why Comic Book Café was a safe haven for me. The bullies never came to Comic Book Café. Their disinterest in comic books was a stroke of luck for me.

In fact, there weren't many students at our school who enjoyed reading comic books. Most of the students in my class didn't visit Comic Book Café. Even though I spent a lot of time there, I rarely ran into any fellow students. I was fortunate in that regard. If word had spread that I frequented Comic Book Café, the bullies might have come looking for me. My only peaceful wish during that time was to be out of sight of my fellow students.

However, it didn't take long for one of my classmates to find me in the Comic Book Café. I encountered my classmate at Comic Book Café. When I met my classmate in the comic book store, a worry crossed my mind. It was the fear that the rumor of me going to Comic Book Café would spread among my classmates.

However, my worries disappeared not long after. Fortunately, the girl I encountered at Comic Book Café was not a bad person. I used to call her the 'manga girl'. She, too, was one of the people who had experienced bullying.

The manga girl had a quite challenging life at school, even more so than I did, to be honest. I was a boy, and she was a girl. The groups that bullied us were different. I was bullied by male bullies, and she was bullied by female bullies. She and I both didn't like our school.

I knew why people bullied her. People who share similar hardships tend to recognize each other. The manga girl had white flakes growing from her hair. People thought it was dandruff when they saw it. I didn't know much about it until I got a closer look one day, and I noticed it. However, those white flakes growing from her hair weren't because she lacked hygiene. When I walked by her once, I noticed a very pleasant scent coming from her. Her hair wasn't greasy at all. It looked as if she had just washed it a few hours ago. I learned then that those white flakes were just a physical trait of hers.

But the bullies weren't interested in her condition. They just assumed that she wasn't clean and kept harassing her. Her situation was horrific. The bullies who tormented her also targeted anyone who befriended her. Consequently, she couldn't become friends with anyone in the class.

I was also a victim of bullying. However, the bullies who tormented me only targeted me, not those I associated with. I had a few other classmates who were victims of bullying in our class. With several victims of bullying in our class, I formed close bonds. Bullied individuals usually weren't mean to others, so they got along easily. I managed to become close to the other male victims of bullying in our class. They weren't entirely devoid of social skills. When we grouped together, we got along quite well.

But even so, we couldn't become close friends with the manga girl. It felt awkward because of the gender difference. If I had tried to befriend girls back then and got rejected, I would have become a laughingstock. Looking back now, I wonder why I cared so much about what others thought. It didn't really matter how people perceived me. I guess I was quite immature back then.

Anyway, when I first encountered the manga girl at the comic book store, she quickly borrowed a manga and left the store. She seemed uncomfortable around me. I wasn't entirely comfortable either when I first met her. I was someone who found it difficult to be around other classmates. Thus, I was glad that she left quickly.

However, that discomfort gradually faded with time. We kept running into each other at the Comic Book Café. She didn't want to make me feel uncomfortable. Her consideration continued, and I began to trust her. I was convinced that she wouldn't do anything to harm me.

As we spent more time together, our relationship began to change. Sometimes, we would make eye contact without tension. Occasionally, she would also read manga at Comic Book Café while I was in Comic Book Café. We didn't read manga together intimately. We weren't that close yet. We simply coexisted without interfering in each other's activities. Nevertheless, witnessing each other enjoying our respective pastimes in the same space was something we hadn't seen before.

Once she became more comfortable, I greeted her briefly when we crossed paths at Comic Book Café.

"Hello."

It was a simple greeting, without any ulterior motives. After all, there shouldn't be any issue with saying hello, I thought.

But it seemed to be a surprising shock to her. She looked at me with larger eyes than when she first saw me at Comic Book Café. I was nervous too, to the point where I could feel the tension.

However, she soon responded with a calm look and said, "Hello."

That's how we began exchanging greetings with each other.

CHAPTER 3

●●●

Since that day, we became at least on speaking terms when we crossed paths. We weren't that close. We were only friends who just exchanged greetings whenever we saw each other. We were more like neighbors. Still, we didn't ignore each other, so at least I felt a fairly deep connection with her. The school's bullies tormented students by harming the things they loved the most.

However, there was an issue that arose one day at the Comic Book Café. It wasn't a problem between her and me; it was simply an issue of not being able to borrow the comic book I really wanted. It wasn't a major problem, to be honest.

The biggest event at the Comic Book Café was the release of new volumes, especially those of highly popular series. The most popular genre in the Comic Book Café wasn't action or comedy but new volumes. Borrowing new volumes was a competitive endeavor because many people wanted to get their hands on them. Sometimes, I had to wait for weeks for my turn to come around. So, if I spotted a new volume, I had to borrow it right away because missing the chance could mean waiting a long time for the next opportunity.

I was deeply immersed in comic books at the time, to the point where new releases would get me overly excited. I would lose my composure, not that I had much composure to begin with. However, I wasn't the only one like this. Other people were just as passionate about comic books, and seeing a new release could make their eyes light up just like mine.

So, in order to win the competition for borrowing new volumes against these people who shared my passion, I needed my own strategy. Others were just as eager to read new volumes as I was, so I had to find a way to outsmart them and make my brain work faster. It was a time to prepare my strategy.

My strategy might not have been anything extraordinary. After all, how much strategy could there be in borrowing comic books? However, surprisingly, even in such situations, having a slight edge in thinking could make a difference. I could create that small difference, and it all began with finding out the release date of the new comic books.

Once someone borrowed a new volume of a comic book, I never knew when they would return it. There was no fixed time for returns; the person just had to bring it back within three days from the day he borrowed it, as per the Comic Book Café 's rules. Sometimes people would return it the very next day, other times it would take them three days, or they might keep it for a week and pay the overdue fee.

In simple terms, once someone borrowed a comic book, I couldn't know when it would come back. So, it was crucial to borrow the new release before anyone else did.

The strategy to borrow it before someone else was indeed

possible. It just required waiting at the Comic Book Café on the day the new volumes were delivered.

I was close with the owner of the Comic Book Café. I practically lived there almost every day. So, the Comic Book Café was like my second home, and the owner who ran it was like my another family member.

I used to ask her when the new volumes would arrive. She was the one who ordered comic books for the store, so she had that information. She was always willing to share it, especially with regular customers like me. Why would she refuse when a loyal customer wanted to borrow comic books?

With the help of the owner, I could always know in advance when the new volumes would arrive. So, on the day of the release, I would rush to the Comic Book Café after school. I wanted to be there as early as possible to wait for the new releases.

Then one day, I happened to be on cleaning duty at school. Being on cleaning duty meant that I had to clean the classrooms after school. It was a role assigned to different students on a rotating basis as per the school rules. Our school believed that students should take care of their own classrooms since they were considered the owners of their respective classes.

The problem was that the day I had cleaning duty happened to coincide with the arrival of a new volume of my favorite manga.

At that time, the most famous manga was the story of pirates. It was about a strange guy who wore a straw hat and accidentally ate a strange fruit that turned his body into rubber. When his body changed, instead of going to the hospital, he set off on a journey. Inside the manga, there was a mysterious island, and if someone arrived there, he could find all the world's treasures and become the king of the pirates. The story of a patient with a rubber body dreaming of becoming the king of the pirates was my favorite manga story. But, of all days, the day I was assigned for the cleaning duty had to be the day the new volume of that manga was released. The god of cleaning duty didn't have mercy. He was more like a pirate.

If the cleaning duty team was focused and worked efficiently, cleaning wouldn't take that long. To be honest, if the team put in a little effort, it wouldn't even take 30 minutes. It mainly involved sweeping the floor and then mopping it. The team also had to clean the windows, but that could be done while someone else was sweeping the floor.

I finished cleaning so quickly that it could have been considered a new world record. If there was a Nobel Prize for cleaning, I would have been the clear winner. It was such a missed opportunity.

I couldn't leave school before I finished my cleaning duty. So, I had to sprint to the Comic Book Café as soon as my cleaning duty was over. Sprinting was all I could do to get to the Comic Book Café early.

When I arrived at the Comic Book Café, I was sweating profusely. I had no idea how long it had been since I had sweated so much. I was not a man of sport. Nevertheless, I didn't have time to wipe off the sweat. I went straight to the new release section. I needed to find the comic book I wanted to borrow. But no matter how hard I looked, I couldn't find the comic book I was searching for.

I eventually asked the owner of the store.

"Did someone already borrow the comic book I was looking for?"

With her usual cheerful voice, the owner replied, "Yes!"

My backpack always had comic books in it. Taking out and reading comic books during break time was my daily routine.

I heard that when a smoker starts quitting, they experience withdrawal symptoms. Similarly, when I couldn't read the comic books I wanted, it felt like I was experiencing withdrawal symptoms. An inexplicable anxiety came over me. I heard that people who suffer severe withdrawal symptoms can even feel like bugs are crawling on their bodies. After experiencing some withdrawal symptoms, I felt like if the symptoms got worse, such things could actually happen.

Before discovering the joy of comic books, whenever I had nothing to do, I used to stroll through the park and indulge in pleasant daydreams. However, after diving into comic books, I found that strolling through the park and indulging in pleasant daydreams no longer felt enjoyable. It seemed that humans lose interest in hobbies they once loved when they find something more enjoyable.

However, I couldn't dwell on the situation of not being able to read comic books. As time passed, the sun set, the moon rose, and the next day arrived. With the arrival of a new day, I had to go to school once again, and I had to forget about yesterday's events. So, when the next day arrived, I became a student once again and headed to school.

When I arrived in my class, I sat down on my seat and checked if I had forgotten any homework, as I often did. I was really bad at staying organized, so I would often forget to bring my homework. This level of forgetfulness qualified me as a sufferer of social anxiety disorder, I suppose.

If there were no lingering homework in my mind, I would start doodling in my notebook. I had nothing else to do. I did have a few friends, but we didn't hang out much. We just socialized when we went to have lunch.

I got up for a moment to throw away some trash. The trash bin was located at the back of the classroom. While heading towards the bin, I passed by a familiar face. It was the manga girl.

The manga girl was sitting near the trash bin. We had started greeting each other in the manga store, and we even exchanged greetings at school. I didn't know what the criteria for friends are, but was this enough to call us friends? I wasn't the type to ask, 'Are we friends?' to anyone, but I guess everyone felt that way.

I was just going to pass by this time without saying anything. Throwing away the trash was my first priority. Still, I noticed that she was looking at something. It was a manga, no bigger than what one could hold with one hand. It couldn't be anything else.

Comic books were strictly prohibited at school back then. However, I couldn't blame the manga girl for bringing the comic book to the school. I was also someone who brought comic books to school. If I didn't, it would actually seem strange to the teachers. They caught me bringing comic books too many time, that it became a daily routine for me.

Anyway, the manga girl reading a banned comic book at school was a bit of shock. She seemed like the type who would never cause any trouble at school. She seemed like a good kid.

However, I was bit relieved at the fact that she was doing what she wanted to do. She always looked so timid and didn't express her own opinion. I sometimes wished that she could do or say what she wanted. People didn't have to be the ones that the others asked to be.

In that sense, I looked at her reading a comic book positively. She was doing something she liked.

I approached her without much thought and struck up a conversation.

"Is that a comic book?" I asked.

The comic girl looked at me with surprise. I could tell from her body language that she was taken aback from the moment I started talking to her. However, I had no intention of bothering her. I was simply curious and wanted to ask a question to someone I was familiar with.

And she responded to my question.

"Yeah."

Come to think of it, it was the first time we exchanged words other than a simple "hello." Could it be that our relationship had evolved from acquaintances to friends?

I nodded in response to her answer. Then, I tried to go back to my seat. There was no particular reason for me to talk to her, just curiosity about her actions had arisen. Now that my curiosity had been satisfied, I was about to return to my seat.

However, as I was walking back to my seat, one of the characters from the comic book she had been reading caught my eye. It was a pirate with a straw hat on his head, a character who could stretch his body like rubber and hadn't been to the hospital for inspection. The comic it appeared in was my favorite.

I had read that comic countless times. I knew it so well that I could recite almost every scene by heart. While I couldn't remember a single thing from all the textbooks I had ever studied, I could remember everything about that comic.

But the comic she was reading was different. Although it featured characters I loved, it depicted scenes I had never seen before.

'It's a new release,' I realized in an instant. The person who had borrowed the comic book before me was none other than the comic girl.

I really wanted to read that new release. So, I wanted to ask the comic girl if I could borrow it. But there was one problem. I wasn't really good at talking to the others. Asking someone for a favor wasn't something I had tried before. So, I was unsure if it would be okay to ask her a favor. I didn't want to bother her and risk making her uncomfortable.

I contemplated the nature of our relationship. If we were already friends, then it would be reasonable to make such a request. However, we weren't quite at that stage yet.

'Were we friends?'

It was a question that crossed my mind. Maybe we were, or maybe we weren't. It was too early to tell.

Nonetheless, I really wanted to read that new release. So, I was trying to think of a way to ask her politely if I could borrow it. But I couldn't come up with a good approach.

Suddenly, her unexpected question resolved my dilemma.

"Do you want to read it too?"

She sensed my dilemma without me saying a word. She was willing to grant my unspoken wish. I felt a bit awkward about the situation. It wasn't common for someone to extend kindness to me.

So, I asked her, "Can I read it too?"

She responded with a bright smile, "Sure!"

The comic girl handed me the newly released comic book she had borrowed. I was surprised. I didn't know how to respond when someone showed kindness like that. I thanked her, not sure what more to do. But it seemed like she was fine with just a simple thank you.

Pure kindness was unfamiliar to me, and I didn't know how to react. It was a confusing day.

Once, I remember doing homework for our ethics class. I'm not sure if they have ethics class in other countries. I've been studying in the United States since high school, but I hadn't encountered ethics class in the country.

Ethics class was different from ordinary classes. It was a time to reflect and discuss morally challenging situations. It didn't discuss history or math. There was no right answer that the ethics class required. Most of the work I had to do in the class was to discuss intriguing topics.

One of the most intriguing topics was about conflicts we might face in our own lives, like family issues.

'What should I do if I witness a family member committing a crime when I was a police officer?'

It was one of the questions that was given in the class. If it was my sister committing a crime, I would insist on strict punishment and report it right away. I would even tell the press to make it a huge issue. Then I'd go home and tease her about it. She might try to beat me with a golf club once more, but it would have been worth it. But what if it was my parent or brother who committed the crime? I had to think about what I was going to do once more.

That question consumed an entire class session. In truth, it wasn't a very difficult question. If someone witnesses a family member committing a crime, he could report it as a citizen and advocate for him as a family member. Sometimes, difficult questions were solved with simple answers. Regardless, pondering such questions was the essence of our ethics class.

However, ethics class was a class. It had exams and homework too. It wasn't just about discussions and contemplation.

One of the assignments was to write a personal essay in response to questions posed by the teacher. These questions were written on different pages of a booklet, and we had to fill in the answers on the remaining pages as our homework.

Honestly, filling in the content for the questions wasn't that difficult. If I took some time to think about it at home, I could easily come up with essay topics. However, the quantity of the assignments was quite substantial, so it wasn't something I could complete during a break. Therefore, the most important thing in ethics class homework was not to forget that I had homework. Unfortunately, for me, that was the most challenging part.

Luckily, I didn't forget about my ethics class homework too often. The homework sheets were pieces of paper, and when I put them in my backpack, I would be reminded of the homework every time I opened my bag. While looking for other textbooks, I'd come across that sheet and think, "Oh right, I have homework!" As a result, I could finish most of the ethics homework in time.

One day, during a break before ethics class, I had finished all my homework and was getting ready for ethics class. Then, an unexpected visitor arrived. It was a big kid who normally had no interest in me whatsoever.

"Did we have homework?" the big kid asked me.

The big kid looked somewhat like one of the bullies. He was just as physically imposing as them. However, he wasn't a bully. Unlike the bullies who didn't study much, the big kid valued his grades.

He thought that befriending them wouldn't benefit his future. So, he kept his distance from the bullies. Interestingly, he kept distance from outsiders, like me, as well. He considered that befriending them wouldn't benefit his life, either. As a result, the big kid didn't have a close relationship with me.

But that day, the big kid was talking to me for some reason.

"Is that homework? Did we have homework?"

The big kid asked. I wasn't sure how to respond. There was homework, but it seemed like the big kid hadn't done it. So, it was difficult for me to say, "Yes, there was homework." It might come across as, "Didn't you do your homework?"

I simply nodded without saying much.

"Yeah."

I was trying to be considerate of him. By reminding him that there was homework, I didn't want to dig into his sore spot. For a kid who hadn't done his homework, the most painful question would be, "Did you do your homework?" So, I tried to respond to his question as politely as possible.

He asked me urgently, "Can I see your homework?"

Ethics class dealt with ethics, and showing my homework to someone else wasn't ethically sound. However, considering how urgently the big kid seemed to need help, I couldn't refuse his request. He looked genuinely distressed, as if not doing the homework would be a big problem for him. Moreover, I was already a kid who used to bring comic book to the school no matter how hard my teachers told me not to. Thus, I didn't think showing him my homework as a huge issue.

Still, I did feel a bit uncomfortable about showing my homework. The big kid had ignored me when I asked for help with my homework before. Still, knowing how painful it could be to not do homework, I decided to be kind and let him see mine.

However, there was one problem. There wasn't much time left until ethics class started. The homework was quite extensive. Completing it during the break wasn't possible.

Nevertheless, I told the big kid that he could take a look at my homework. I hoped it would be of some help to him. But he realized there wasn't much time left either. After some contemplation, he decided not to take my homework and returned to his seat.

It felt disappointing that I couldn't help the big kid. However, I didn't have much time to think about it. The class was about to start soon, so I wanted to prepare for it. I hadn't had the chance to talk to the big kid. Instead, I chose to go to the restroom. I didn't want a kid squeezing his leg during class time.

I hurriedly went to the restroom. Fortunately, I could return before the class started. I quickly returned to my seat. The class was about to begin shortly, as the bell was about to ring.

However, a problem arose. My homework that had been on my desk had disappeared.

Panic set in. I tried to remember where I might have put it, but I couldn't recall anything except leaving it on my desk. I hadn't moved it anywhere else.

I checked everywhere, but I couldn't find my homework. For a moment, I had a worrying thought that someone might have done something bad to me, taken my homework intentionally. I thought someone was trying to fool me. It wasn't good to suspect others without any evidence, but for some reason, the suspicion didn't go away. If someone didn't take it, my homework shouldn't be missing.

I thought about where I might have placed my homework if someone wanted to play a prank on me. And there was one place that came to mind—the trash bin.

I rushed to the trash bin. Maybe someone maliciously threw my homework in there. At that moment, I was desperate. The class was about to start, and I was almost certain that I would receive a zero for not having my homework. So honestly, if I could just find my homework and turn it in on time, I wouldn't care who discarded it. I just wanted to submit my assignment when it was needed.

But I couldn't find my homework in the trash bin. However, I didn't have much time to continue searching. I had to return to my seat. The class was about to start, and not being in my seat when the class began was sure to cause trouble.

When I almost gave up searching, I turned towards the window. Our classroom had a small terrace right outside the window. The terrace was too narrow for a person to climb onto; it was more like a tiny space with a few small potted plants. It was about the length of my arm.

No one really paid much attention to that terrace. In fact, we often wondered why it was there. Perhaps it was for decoration, I thought a few times. I even wanted to ask someone about its purpose, but I doubted anyone would know. It seemed that even the principal might not have known the true nature of that terrace.

However, there was one moment when students used the terrace—the moment when they disposed of trash. There was a trash bin right next to the door leading to the hallway from our classroom. The windows were on the opposite side of the classroom. So, students near the windows had to walk to the hallway on the other side if they wanted to use the trash bin. Our classroom wasn't very big, so it wasn't a big hassle. But some students found it inconvenient and would secretly toss their trash onto the terrace. No one paid attention to that place, so they thought they could get away with it.

I wanted to check the terrace. At this point, it was the only place in the classroom where I hadn't looked. If my homework wasn't on the terrace, it wasn't in the classroom.

However, there was no sign of my homework on the terrace either. I looked around with a sense of disappointment. Still, as I was about to avert my gaze from the terrace, something caught my eye. It was a torn piece of paper, specifically a torn edge of a paper bundle.

For some reason, that torn edge of paper looked familiar to me. The texture and color of the paper were ones I had seen many times before.

I approached it and examined it more closely. Fortunately, it was within reach if I stretched my hand out through the window. I reached out and picked up the object.

It turned out to be a part of my homework. The torn edge had my name and the words "Ethics Class Homework" written on it.

It was clear that someone had torn off the part with my name from my homework and taken it. I brought that torn edge with my name back to my seat. It was difficult to control my anger. No matter how much I thought about it, it seemed unlikely that anyone would have a reason to tear someone else's homework like that.

However, a strange feeling crept in as I regained my composure. Specifically, not many people knew the fact that I had done my homework. In that moment, I looked at one person in the classroom, and it was the big kid.

No matter how much I thought about it, it didn't seem like many people would tear up my homework like that. Even the bullies didn't mess with my homework. They tried to avoid causing any trouble with the teachers. So, they didn't engage in actions that would disrupt others' studies, or they might face continuous reprimands from the teachers.

Therefore, the only possible culprit I could think of was the one who had asked me if I had homework. I didn't want to rashly think that the big kid had taken my homework. However, the suspicion lingered.

Then, the moment of confirmation arrived. I witnessed the big kid with my own eyes, holding completed homework he hadn't done. He had to be the one who stole my homework.

Our school teachers were never late. The ethics teacher, in particular, always arrived before the bell rang. On that day as well, our ethics teacher had arrived promptly, just as usual. As soon as the ethics teacher entered the classroom, the request was straightforward: submit homework.

Most students got up from their seats and gathered around the ethics teacher, each holding their prepared homework. They were the ones who could avoid getting a zero in the homework section of their report cards.

However, there were a few students who didn't get up from their seats. They were the ones without the homework. But I didn't have time to focus on them. I realized something more important. I hadn't gotten up from my seat, and the big kid was submitting the homework.

Just a while ago, the big kid had asked for my help because he hadn't done his homework. But now, he magically finished his homework and was submitting the homework, seemingly out of nowhere.

I became convinced that the big kid had taken my homework. There was no way he could finish his homework during a short period of time before the class.

Still, I couldn't confront him without solid evidence. Accusing someone without proper evidence was not the right thing to do. Thus, I wanted to at least see what he was submitting. After all, he had claimed that he hadn't done the homework. I was curious to know how he had managed to complete several pages of it during the break.

I made a plan. If he truly stole my homework, I was going to ask the ethics teacher for help. I would explain my situation and ask the ethics teacher to check just this once if the big kid had actually done the homework.

I watched as the big kid approached our ethics teacher and submitted the homework. Then, I rushed over to the ethics teacher. It was time to take on the role of a detective. As the big kid submitted his homework, I immediately approached the ethics teacher and explained my situation.

"Teacher, I need your help."

I requested assistance from the ethics teacher. At that moment, the only person who could resolve my situation was him.

I tried to explain the situation as calmly as possible. So, I continued speaking.

"Someone has taken my homework. Look at this torn part of my homework. Someone tore off the section with my name and left it on the terrace."

I showed the ethics teacher the torn part of my homework. It was a small, insignificant scrap of paper with only my name and the assignment title written on it. But it was essential evidence for me. It could be used to prove that I had done my homework, and someone had taken it.

The big kid couldn't hide his surprise when he saw me approaching. However, he was quick on his feet. He knew that if he were caught stealing homework, there would be severe consequences.

The ethics teacher, unaware of the situation, wanted a more detailed explanation. So, he asked me, "Did you submit your homework?"

I replied honestly, "No, someone took my homework. I suspect someone, though. It's the big kid. He couldn't finish his homework until just before the class started and asked me for help. But now, I see that he has already completed it and is trying to submit it. It's impossible to complete the homework during the break. It was quite extensive."

As I started explaining the situation, the words I wanted to say flowed out like a torrent. Moreover, my explanation was logical and well-structured, even to my own surprise.

I emphasized that I didn't want to accuse someone without proper evidence. Still, I wanted to ask the ethics teacher to check how the big kid managed to finish the homework so quickly. Thus, I respectfully requested the ethics teacher's assistance and explained the situation, hoping the teacher would understand. Teachers usually listened reasonable student concerns, after all.

Strangely, the ethics teacher seemed rather annoyed. It was as if the ethics teacher wished I would just go back to my seat. The ethics teacher wore a look of impatience, as if wanting the class to start.

The ethics teacher asked me, "What do you want me to do?"

I replied honestly, "Please let me check the big kid's homework just once. I know my handwriting. Thus, I can determine if his homework is mine by looking at it. If it's not my homework, I'll return to my seat. But if it turns out to be mine, I'd like to get it back because I need to submit it."

When I asked to check the big kid's homework, he resisted vigorously. He even shouted, "Get lost, bastard!" in front of the ethics teacher. Most students would never dare to curse in front of their teachers; it could get them into serious trouble. However, the big kid didn't seem to care about what the ethics teacher thought.

But I couldn't back down. This was a moment I couldn't afford to miss. If I stepped back, I could end up with a zero for not submitting my homework.

The ethics teacher, after assessing the situation, asked me to provide the torn part of the homework I had found on the terrace. The teacher also asked the big kid to present his homework for examination.

When the ethics teacher reviewed the big kid's homework, there was a torn section that matched the piece I had brought. All my doubts were cleared in that moment.

"It matches. This is your homework," the ethics teacher declared.

The ethics teacher acknowledged that the homework the big kid had submitted was indeed mine. He asked the big kid if he had his homework. The big kid said that he didn't have his homework. As a result, the ethics teacher gave him a zero score.

It was a moment of justice served, and I felt triumphant. I gave a piercing look to the big kid. I had tried to help him, but he had disappointed me like this. If I were three times his size, I would have given him a piece of my mind.

However, the teacher's next words towards me caught me by surprise: "You also get a zero."

I couldn't understand what he said. I thought the ethics teacher had made a mistake. I explained once again that the homework the big kid had submitted was, in fact, mine. I was willing to submit the homework that I got back.

Still, the ethics teacher didn't take my homework somehow. I believed the ethics teacher had misunderstood. I even mentioned that I had done the homework and was willing to submit it.

But the ethics teacher gave a curt response, "You get a zero. Go back to your seat."

The ethics teacher's face had turned red with anger. It dawned on me that something was seriously wrong.

The ethics teacher had never been interested in finding out who had stolen my homework from the beginning. The teacher just wished that students wouldn't bother and annoy him. That's why the ethics teacher's anger was directed at me, who had caused trouble. I was just an inconvenience to the ethics teacher. I wasn't a student the ethics teacher cared about.

In the end, I received a zero for my homework. I couldn't understand why. What had I done wrong to deserve such treatment?

Honestly, the big kid didn't lose anything. He got a zero, but he hadn't done the homework in the first place. So, receiving a zero meant nothing to him.

On the other hand, I felt like a fool. I had done my homework, only for it to be stolen. I had finally caught the thief and retrieved my homework, but I still received a zero.

I wondered why I had even bothered trying so hard. The ethics teacher didn't even take any action against the big kid, despite clear evidence of theft. It was a confusing and frustrating experience. The world was a difficult place to understand.

During my middle school years, there were a lot of people to harm me. Still, there wasn't anyone to protect me. School wasn't a home, and teachers weren't my parents. I felt like a wild animal surviving alone in a safari. It would have been nice to have a strong friend, like a rhinoceros, but I had very few friends, and most of them weren't huge and didn't have a horn on their nose. I sometimes wished I could be as strong as a rhinoceros, but , I felt more like a sloth. It felt like hyenas were ready to pounce on me at any moment.

Going to school felt like walking through a minefield every day. A single mistake could trigger an explosion. I had a knack for getting into trouble in unexpected ways.

I used to think that being kind to others would bring goodness back to me. However, there were times when my attempts to help others resulted in unfavorable outcomes, and I ended up with bruises, both physically and emotionally.

One day, I found abandoned homework in the classroom and returned it to its owner. To my surprise, the owner complained about why there were stains on their homework. I had just picked it up from the floor and handed it back as it was. I tried to explain, but all I got in return was a powerful punch.

I got used to this strange world. I realized that I didn't have to understand everything about the world. I began to wish that as long as there were no problems, I'd be content. I learned to let go of bewildering incidents without dwelling on them. Deep thinking didn't yield any benefits. I just accepted whatever happened with a "so be it" attitude. Even if someone treated me unfairly, I didn't feel the need to express my discontent. I thought that being obedient and avoiding trouble was the best course of action.

Perhaps, unknowingly, I was becoming like the ethics teacher.

All the effort to overcome my situation seemed futile. Maybe the ethics teacher was once a person full of dreams and hopes but had changed due to unfortunate circumstances. Thinking about it, I could understand the ethics teacher's heart. If only I were a little older, I might have been able to protect the ethics teacher. It's something I regret.

I was eager for the environment I was in to come to an end, especially my middle school years. I had grown tired of the environment I lived in. I really disliked middle school.

And someone simply offered me a act of kindness.

"Do you want to see it too?"

A girl in the same class who shared my interest in manga showed me a manga book I liked. I hadn't done anything for her. I couldn't expect what she wanted in return. Interestingly, she didn't want something back from me. She just wanted me to enjoy the comics.

I guessed that the middle school could be somewhere enjoyable. I hoped that she could enjoy her school life as well, since she made me enjoy it.

The manga girl seemed like a good person. I hoped a bright future awaited her.

But my wish didn't come true. After few weeks, she jumped from the school building and never returned.

During my middle school days, we had short breaks after each class. Each class was 50 minutes, and the breaks were only 10 minutes long.

During those breaks, kids always gathered with their close friends. The short 10-minute break was not wasted. People chatted, laughed, and shared moments with their friends.

However, I didn't particularly socialize with my friends during those breaks. I preferred walking around alone rather than mingling with others. Being alone was the most comfortable for me. My lack of social skills was quite severe.

Unlike me, the manga girl didn't spend her breaks alone either. She didn't have friends in our class, but a friend from another class often came to find her during breaks. I used to call the friend as 'glasses girl.' She was a girl who was bullied in her class. That's why she came to see the manga girl all the time. She didn't like to spend time in her class.

The glasses girl and the manga girl had a special ability. When the glasses girl stood in front of our classroom, the manga girl somehow knew she had arrived, even if she hadn't been called. And when the glasses girl came, the manga girl immediately left.

It wouldn't have been a problem if they played in our classroom. I never heard of any rule that students from other classes couldn't come into our classroom. However, the glasses girl and the manga girl always went outside. They would come back to the classroom around the end of the break time. Sometimes, I wondered where they went, but I never really tried to find out. I didn't think they wanted the others to know too much detail about them.

In contrast to them, I often spent my time alone. If I got bored, I would go to the school store. There was a small store near the school entrance. Normally, the students weren't supposed to leave the school until it was time to go home, but the store was inside the school. It was right next to the main school gate, attached to it. Thanks to that, students could use it during break times or lunchtime.

The school store didn't have a wide variety of items for sale, especially not school supplies. For some reason, the store focused on selling snacks rather than school supplies. If they had sold school supplies at the store, the owner would have become rich. Why didn't they sell school supplies at the store?

There were cookies and drinks, and there were plenty of bread in the school store. The bread sold at the store was all produced in a factory, so it was reasonably priced. If an official baker cooked the bread, it had to be expensive. It's hard to describe the taste. It was just incredibly sweet. It must have had a lot of sugar in it. It was so sweet that it felt like my teeth would rot with each bite. I was sure that the factory used more sugar than flour.

However, personally, those overly sweet school store pastries were perfect for me. I didn't have much money, and I was someone who liked sweeter pastries. So the school store pastries that provided sweetness on a tight budget were the best choice for me. I was overweight at the time. Sugar was as important to me as water. Sometimes, I even brought cola in my water bottle. Drinking cola in front of the teacher, pretending it was water, was like a pop in my mouth. Maybe it was because of the carbonation?

The school store sold a variety of pastries. Among them, my favorite was the chocolate-flavored roll cake. However, it was so popular that it sold out quickly. The pastries I bought often came with stickers. They were cute character stickers. Some of my classmates would give away the pastries to other friends and just collect the stickers. There were people who filled half their notebooks with stickers. But I wasn't really interested in stickers, so I usually just threw them away. I wonder if I should have given them to a friend who collected stickers?

School store wasn't that far from my classroom. It took less than 5 minutes to walk from my classroom to the school store. I never measured it exactly, but I just had a sense that it was about that far. Usually, when I returned from the school store, it was almost the end of break time. Of course, that meant I didn't have a separate time to eat the pastries. So, I usually ate the pastries on my way back to the classroom. I was a fast eater, so it wasn't a problem.

For some reason, I felt good after eating something while

passing the time. Sweet food had the power to make me happy. I should definitely consider replacing my teeth with marshmallows when I grow up.

But one day, something happened. It was no different from any other day when I went to the school store.

Usually, when I came back from school store, most of the kids were seated. It was time to start preparing for class. Some kids had already opened their textbooks. When that happened, I quickly returned to my seat. Like the other kids, I opened my textbook and took my seat. After that, my job was to quickly wipe away any bread crumbs from around my mouth.

However, that day, I saw a strange scene. Even though I had returned to the classroom, almost none of the students were sitting in their seats. At first, I thought maybe I had gone to the school store too quickly. Since it wasn't time for class to start yet, I thought the students weren't in their seats yet. But when I checked the clock, I realized that class was about to start soon.

I still tried to return to my seat. Others not sitting on their seat didn't mean I couldn't. Time would pass, the clock hands would move, and the class would start.

However, something caught my eye as I attempted to return to my seat. It was the students gathered by the window.

I couldn't quite figure out why they were huddled there. There were so many people crowded together that I couldn't see what was in front of them. All I could see were the backs of people who were looking at something outside the window.

At first, I also tried to look outside. I wanted to see what they were seeing. After all, when people are all looking at something, it arouses curiosity, doesn't it?

But there were too many students by the window. They were packed so tightly that there was no space in between. I almost believed that they had found a Tinker Bell. What else could draw their attention so badly?

If I had been closer to the students in my class, I might have just grabbed one of them by the window and asked what they were looking at. But I wasn't very close to most of my classmates, so I was cautious about approaching the students by the window.

In the end, I looked outside through another window in the classroom. Initially, I thought that there must be someone outside that the students were gathering to see. But I couldn't find anything outside when I saw through another window. There was just the dusty sand field, as always.

It was then that I realized that the students were surrounding just one window for some reason. Even though there were more windows in the classroom, they were all huddled around this single window. There seemed to be a reason for it.

However, I couldn't figure out the reason. So, I decided to go back to my seat. The students around the window didn't seem like they were going to make room for me. Moreover, I didn't want to risk annoying them by trying to get a better view.

Fortunately, I got a chance to see what was outside the window. It was finally time for class to start. The students who had been standing by the window started returning to their seats.

Through the gap between the students by the window, I saw what was outside the window. It was none other than my dear friend, the manga girl.

Outside our classroom window, there was a narrow terrace. It was so narrow that it was a dangerous space for someone to stand. If someone took a wrong step, something he'd rather not think about could happen. It was the same terrace where I had found a portion of my torn-up homework. For some reason, the manga girl was standing on the narrow terrace outside.

At first, I couldn't understand what was happening. Until now, no one had ever gone out onto the terrace. Anyone would know that going onto the terrace was extremely dangerous. Kids like me couldn't even stand there because our legs would tremble.

But for some reason, the manga girl was standing there on the terrace without moving a muscle. She seemed frozen.

I couldn't fathom why she had gone out onto the terrace. But now, I was starting to feel afraid. I didn't like the idea of my friend being in a dangerous situation.

I wanted to persuade her directly. I wanted to tell her to come back to the classroom now that it was time for class. All she had to do was step back inside through the window. It was just one step away. I wanted to talk to her to make that one step.

I began to approach the window. I wanted to calmly persuade her from up close. I didn't want to shout at her from a distance, as it would have been risky. She was in a very dangerous situation. She must have been quite shocked. Shouting at her might startle her, and in a dangerous place like the terrace, she might lose her balance. That could lead to a terrible accident.

So, I wanted to speak to her calmly.

"It'll be okay. Nothing's going to happen."

I wanted to deliver a reassuring message as if I were transmitting these words to her. I didn't want to see my friend flustered. I just wanted her to be happy. That's why I wanted to speak with a calm voice by her side.

I began to inch closer to the window. I wanted to talk to her with a smiling face.

But when I had come close enough to speak to her through the window, I saw the presence of some students. They were the bullies, precisely the ones who had tormented her and the ones who had tormented me.

At first, I didn't pay much attention to them. I just wanted to say a word to my friend. But then, I noticed their expressions. I couldn't look away from them.

They were laughing heartily while looking at the manga girl. I couldn't understand what was so amusing. The manga girl was standing precariously on the terrace. For some reason, they found it entertaining. I couldn't comprehend why they were reacting this way. If I were in their shoes, I would have tried to help the girl who loved comics.

It was only then that I realized the bullies were the ones who had pushed my friend into that dangerous place, the terrace.

The people who threatened my friend were none other than the ones I had always feared the most. It was the first time I felt such intense anger towards those bullies. I was surprised by the fact that I could muster that much anger within myself. I had always felt powerless, but that didn't matter now. I wanted to save my friend; I wanted to approach her and ignore those bullies for the moment. I wanted to rescue her.

However, a terrifying thought suddenly crossed my mind. It was a chilling idea that made me freeze with fear.

'What if I rescue the manga girl, and then the bullies turn against me?'

The moment that thought surfaced, I couldn't move. Bullies despised being interrupted when they were up to their mischief. If such a situation arose, they always sought revenge in some wicked way.

My entire body felt stiff. It seemed like my blood pressure was rising, and my heart was pounding intensely. I briefly turned my head away from the manga girl and looked at the bullies. They were the ones I had always dreaded.

The bullies were tormenting the manga girl. I wanted to confront them to save her.

But then, a new worry began to creep in.

'What if I get chased out to the terrace next?'

I could see a future I hadn't witnessed yet, where I was powerless and couldn't save the manga girl. Even if I managed to rescue her, there was no guarantee of success. It seemed impossible to defeat that gang of bullies and save her.

However, one thing I was sure of was that they would be uncomfortable with my actions. Their response would be clear-cut. They would turn me into their next target. They could easily achieve that by chasing me out onto the terrace. They would laugh at me, just like they were enjoying the manga girl's suffering.

Of course, their retaliatory actions were just a product of my imagination. Still, I was paralyzed by that thought. It felt like that grim future was inevitable.

My steps toward my friend halted. My concern for her crumbled.

Still, when I thought I had to muster the courage, another thought crossed my mind.

'What if I get chased out to the terrace, and there's no one to help me?'

From that moment on, I felt like my face was turning pale because I already knew the answer. When the manga girl was chased out to the terrace, no one came to her aid. How could I even entertain the thought that someone would help me in the same situation?

I could feel the vitality draining from my face. I glanced around the classroom briefly. My determination to rescue the manga girl underwent a change. Initially, I wanted to approach her to save my friend and have an ordinary day. But now, it seemed like I was becoming self-centered.

'At least I'm not on the terrace right now.'

That was the thought in my head. I didn't need to worry about anything else since I was safe. I looked at the other students who were just indifferent to the manga girl.

'Maybe I could pretend not to be aware of the danger? Perhaps she doesn't know either.'

I was surprised at how effortlessly I justified my own cowardice to myself. That moment stayed with me. I had never felt so repulsed by my own actions before. It felt as if I was about to vomit. There was a sensation as if vomit was flowing through my pores. It felt like I was suffocating due to the intense heat, and my skin was melting away.

I made an effort not to turn away from the manga girl, just standing there near the window. What choice did I have? I couldn't bear to ignore her. However, I still lacked the courage to confront the bullies. But there was no longer any need for a conflict. The moment I imagined my future where I'd be chased out to the terrace, I felt paralyzed. It seemed like that inevitable future was closing in on me.

My steps towards my friend came to a halt. My concern for her crumbled. And, the moment I had to stop conflicting came. The manga girl made the decision to jump off the terrace herself.

CHAPTER 4

• • • •

"Thud!"

A muffled sound came from where the manga girl had fallen. Without hesitation, I rushed to the window. The bullies who had gathered by the window until then looked startled. Suddenly, they returned to their seats. They no longer wanted to be involved in the situation.

I reached the window and looked down at the ground. The manga girl was lying there.

Outside our school building, there was a small garden with grass and trees. The manga girl had landed there. There was no sign of blood. I could see her blinking her eyes. Fortunately, she was alive.

At that moment, screams were heard from a distance. Perhaps

someone outside the school had accidentally witnessed the manga girl falling. Suddenly, the entire school began to get chaotic.

Right at that time, a teacher for the next class entered the classroom. However, no one but the bullies was in their seats. Most of the classmates had gathered by the window, looking at the manga girl.

The teacher who had just entered the classroom seemed puzzled. It was understandable since none of the students were prepared for the lesson. Then, one student ran up to the teacher, probably trying to explain the situation.

The teacher listened to the explanation. Then his expression changed dramatically. I didn't know that a teacher could have such a terrifying expression.

The teacher immediately went to the window and saw the manga girl lying on the ground outside. Without saying a word about the class, he quickly rushed out. I didn't realize that even adults could be so flustered.

Most of the students, including myself, stayed by the window, watching over the manga girl. No one said a word.

After a while, several teachers ran towards the manga girl. Even the teacher who had intended to continue our class had somehow run down to the first floor and approached the manga girl.

The manga girl seemed to notice the teachers approaching. She suddenly tried to get up, waving her hand as if to reassure them that she was okay. However, the teachers prevented her from moving at all, firmly instructing her not to move. They stayed by her side, guarding her carefully.

The teachers were trying to prevent any further injury or harm to the manga girl, as she had just fallen from a high place. There could have been invisible injuries.

Soon after, we heard sirens. An ambulance arrived at the school's sports field. That's when the teachers started moving.

Paramedics arrived. The teachers helped them load the manga girl into the ambulance. After the ambulance left the school premises, the teachers began coming into the school one by one.

Even after the manga girl was transported to the hospital, I couldn't forget the image of her lying on the grass. I didn't know what to say to her when she returned. I felt cowardly.

I had avoided the manga girl when she was in danger. I prioritized my own safety. Eventually, she jumped from the school building.

I felt guilty. I wanted to do something for the manga girl, but I didn't know what to do. In the first place, I didn't even know what the manga girl was feeling. When she jumped from the school building and landed on the grass, she didn't show any emotions. I had never experienced the same environment as her, so I couldn't understand her feelings.

I felt partly responsible for what happened to her. It seemed like she jumped because of me.

She was forced to the terrace by the bullies, although I didn't know it at the time. But I had terrifying thoughts. Somehow, it seemed like she jumped because I had avoided her.

Could she have seen my avoidance as a sign that she was unwanted? If there had been at least one person trying to save her, would she not have jumped?

That's when I got really scared. Essentially, my friend seemed to have been driven to despair because of me.

I didn't know how to face my friend. Should I have apologized to her?

But such concerns became meaningless. The manga girl never returned to school.

A few days after the manga girl jumped, homeroom teacher of my classmates and me, who was also our Korean language teacher, informed us about her condition. Fortunately, the manga girl didn't have any life-threatening injuries. However, after the incident, she moved to another school and never returned.

Our homeroom teacher was an excellent educator who led us through understanding rather than just scolding us. I really liked her. She was such a good speaker.

Still, on the day the manga girl fell, our homeroom teacher couldn't bring herself to say anything for a while. She stood in front of the class as if she wanted to say something but couldn't find the words. Eventually, she just mentioned that the manga girl wasn't critically injured and left the room.

After that day, our Korean language teacher started speaking to us less and less. Until then, we had a harmonious relationship with her. However, at some point, it felt like a barrier had formed between us.

Our Korean language teacher would still smile when she greeted us, but for some reason, she stopped looking into our eyes.

I can't forget the first day I met our Korean language teacher. She introduced herself as our homeroom teacher and promised to give us a unique experience. What she had prepared was quite interesting; she decided to teach us the exact meanings of the slang words we often used.

Back then, we students frequently used slang words, even though adults often advised us not to. But our Korean language teacher didn't scold us for using slang. Instead, she encouraged us to write down all the slang words we knew on the chalkboard.

Students began writing down every slang word they knew on the chalkboard. To be honest, it was quite amusing. The mischievous students deliberately wrote down more slang words to see if they could fill up the board. However, our Korean language teacher didn't scold them; she even encouraged them to write more.

Eventually, students ran out of slang words they knew, and some part of the chalkboard remained empty.

When our knowledge of profanity had reached its limits, our Korean language teacher began to speak. She started by pointing out each slang word written on the chalkboard and asked us to look at them. Then she began explaining the meanings of each one. Surprisingly, profanities turned out to be incredibly offensive language. Even the profanities I casually used before had dreadful meanings.

After explaining the meanings of profanities, the teacher went on to explain their origins. Among them, there were some very sad stories. In Korea, there was a term called "horozasik" which was a word used by students in their early years to mock their friends.

Its origin was in a tragic history. Korea had suffered many invasions in the past. Among them, there was a country called the Qing Dynasty that had significant power compared to Korea of that time, known as the Joseon Dynasty. In the 17th century, the Qing Dynasty invaded Joseon. At that time, Korea suffered a humiliating defeat, experiencing the greatest disgrace in its history. To surrender, the Korean king had to kneel three times and kowtow nine times at a place called Samjeondo.

After losing the war, our country had to sell its female citizens as slaves to the Qing Dynasty, calling them "gongnyeo" or palace women. Most of these women returned to Korea after suffering terrible treatment in the Qing Dynasty, many of them coming back pregnant.

These women had done nothing wrong; they were merely sold into slavery because the country lost the war. However, when they returned after suffering the Qing Dynasty's cruelty, they faced an even more tragic reality. People started calling the children of these palace women "horozasik," meaning the children of uncivilized people. "Horozasik" was a derogatory term created to demean the Qing Dynasty's ethnic group, portraying them as a barbaric race. In other words, the children born as a result of rape were not recognized as part of the nation; they were just considered the children of barbarians. Moreover, these palace women ended up being recognized as wives of the barbarians, enemy of the country. They were called concubines of the enemy, despite not having done anything wrong. Moreover, there was no one to understand their suffering and pain. Can anyone imagine how heartbreaking that must have been for them? There was no one to acknowledge their sad reality.

Our Korean language teacher didn't explicitly forbid students from using profanity. However, after students learned the origins of these words, they naturally refrained from using them.

Our Korean language teacher seemed very wise. She trusted the students. So, she believed that if students knew the meanings of profanities, they would naturally refrain from using them. Her judgment was correct. It was better to let students reduce profanities on their own rather than telling them to do so arbitrarily.

However, even such a wise Korean language teacher couldn't handle the aftermath of the manga girl's incident. Korean language teacher couldn't comprehend the pain of the manga girl either. In fact, our Korean language teacher seemed unable to recover from the shock herself. She appeared to struggle with accepting the dire consequences brought about by the students she had believed in. Our Korean language teacher watched over the students and trusted them. But the students showed an incredibly cruel side to the manga girl. Our Korean language teacher may have felt a sense of betrayal.

Students liked our Korean language teacher. So, seeing her disappointed was heartbreaking. Students wanted to apologize for letting down our Korean language teacher. But they couldn't. If an apology were to be made, it should have been directed towards the manga girl.

However, it remains uncertain whether our apology to the manga girl would provide any comfort.

After the incident with the manga girl, there was one change at school. Namely, iron frames were installed on the windows, preventing students from going out onto the terrace. I couldn't understand what the importance of that was. Iron frames didn't seem like they could protect wounded souls.

Before long, my expectations were proven right, even though it should have been okay for them to be wrong. Why did the world want to be so cruel?

After the manga girl didn't come back, sometimes when I read comic books, I would think of her. I used to lend her funny comic books when I had them. She would also show me the comic books she liked. She had a knack for picking out entertaining comic books. There was never a dull one among the comic books I borrowed from her. So, when I realized there was no one to share comic books with, it hit me that she was gone.

After the manga girl left our class, the glasses girl no longer visited. She was the manga girl's only friend. She was a kind girl who would come to our class during breaks, even though she wasn't part of our class. But without the manga girl, there was no reason for her to come to our class anymore.

I wondered how she was dealing with the reality of her friend's disappearance. Did it not matter to her that her friend was gone? In our class, nothing seemed to change after the manga girl's disappearance. Everyone continued with their daily routines as if the manga girl had never been there.

But that couldn't be true. The manga girl had been in our class. The incident that brought her tragic fate into our class was known to everyone. Everyone knew it, and an event happened that made sure everyone knew it. Suddenly, and tragically, just like always.

We were in the middle of a typical day at school, just like any other. All the students were focused on their lessons. The teacher was engrossed in the textbook. Perhaps we had already forgotten about the manga girl. It was the same old classroom scenery we always saw. No matter how tough things were for the manga girl, time had a way of bringing a new day.

Then, someone opened our classroom door abruptly and shouted, "Glasses girl is missing!" The glasses girl had been another student who had suffered bullying along with the manga girl. The news of her disappearance came from the blue-faced teacher of another class.

In that moment, everyone in the classroom was reminded of the past tragedy. It felt like an unimaginable future was creeping in again. Everyone froze, but there was someone quick to make a decision—the teacher, who had been conducting the lesson.

"Everyone, start self-study!" the teacher shouted loudly and immediately left the classroom, exchanging a few words with the teacher from the other class who had reported the glasses girl's disappearance. Then, they rushed off somewhere together.

The remaining students in the class stared at each other. None of us knew how to process the situation.

That's when one student stood up. She had always been the most just girl in our class. She walked out of the class and started calling out the glasses girl's name. She had decided to start looking for her.

WARREN BUFFETT AND THE STREET CLEANER

Our teacher had told us to self-study, meaning to stay seated and study quietly. Disobeying her usually resulted in a sharp reprimand. However, this just girl seemed to disregard that.

Soon after, a few more students started getting up from their seats. There weren't many, but they were students who had decided to take action.

I stood up too. While heading outside, I began calling out the glasses girl's name. The familiar anxiety from the past had returned, as if another tragedy awaited me. It was like a prelude to further tragedy. I shouted the glasses girl's name, just like the others.

Throughout the search for the glasses girl, my uneasiness never left me. I worried that maybe she had also jumped from somewhere. When that fear crept in, I shouted the glasses girl's name even louder. Other students were wrestling with the same concerns because the voices calling for her grew louder from various places.

I felt someone shouting at that moment.

"I found her! She's here!"

It was the discovery of the glasses girl. People started gathering where the sound came from. It was none other than the women's restroom.

I was nearby when the sound occurred, so I quickly arrived at the location.

When I arrived, several children were already there inside the restroom. One of them was calling the teachers.

Many students were coming to the restroom to check on the glasses girl. The restroom door was wide open.

At that moment, I accidentally saw the girl with glasses through the open door. I was shocked by her expression.

The glasses girl was huddled in a corner, crying. Her expression was so devastating that I didn't know how to describe it. I had never seen someone with such an expression before. She had the expression of a dog that had been abused, with tears streaming down her face and trembling.

I had seen videos of abused dogs in the past. They would hide in a corner, looking as if they were about to die, with a pitiful expression. I thought only dogs or animals could make such a miserable expression. I thought civilized people couldn't make a miserable expression like that.

But it was my misconception. People could also make a miserable expression like dogs. People could become as miserable as dogs when they were abused. I didn't know that.

I couldn't hear an explanation for why the glasses girl was crying in the restroom. However, somehow, I understood why she was feeling so hurt. She must have suffered from her friend's disappearance.

It was only then that I could understand the feelings of the manga girl who had jumped off the school building. I thought the manga girl might have had the same feelings as the glasses girl. I just hadn't seen it.

I had to save the manga girl. But it was already too late.

During my middle school years, it wasn't a place where only bad things happened. For example, I still cherish the memories of my Korean language teacher who taught me the meaning of swear words.

However, it was also a place where bad things happened. The incidents involving the manga girl and the glasses girl were prime examples.

After the incident with the glasses girl, there was another disturbance at school not long after. The protagonist of that disturbance was me. Of course, it wasn't a good kind of disturbance. It was the story of me being bullied by bullies and eventually leaving the school. To be more precise, I left the country. I ended up studying in another country because I couldn't adapt to Korean society.

When I reached the third grade of middle school, I ended up in a different class from the one I had been in during my second year. I was still an outcast. Even if I had gone to a different school, I probably would have still been an outcast. Maybe I had a natural talent for being an outcast?

One thing that changed in the third grade was that I had even fewer friends than I did in the second grade. In the new class, I could only be friends with one person.

My only friend was someone who loved making models. He often brought small models to school and assembled them. I called him "Model." It was just a nickname. Still, I personally liked the nickname because it suited him.

Model often brought fascinating things to school. He even brought comic books. In fact, models were just one of the many things he frequently brought. He would also bring gaming magazines and other items. I first learned that game companies published magazines when I saw him bringing them.

Model knew how to enjoy the world much better than I did. At that time, even a comic book store was a shocking place for me. But Model knew about a world even more shocking than that.

He showed me one of the play spaces, which was a game center. It was a place equipped with large gaming machines. We often played games together at the game center. It was great because there were many games for two players. Some games we could enjoy together, but some required us to compete against each other. Whenever we played competitive games, Model would tease me with his strange skills. He was a master at all the games. He never let me win. Sometimes he would pretend to be weak and then turn the tables and beat me. Model didn't go easy on me when it came to competition. He was sometimes a total bastard.

The town where Model lived was far from my house. The atmosphere in his town was quite different from where I lived. So, I always got to see mysterious things that I didn't usually see.

Model's mother was a barber, and his father often did housework. So, when I went to Model's house, his father would often be there. I would greet his father and then play in Model's room. Model always kept a few coins in his room. He usually spent the coins when we went to the game center.

Model didn't have any siblings, so he hung out with me more often. He didn't hesitate to share the allowance he had saved. We often went to the game center together. At the game center, we had to pay for each game we played. But Model always paid for my share. Sometimes, I would insist on paying for my own game, but Model would tell me not to worry about it. So, whenever I went to Model's house to play, I would bring snacks. If I had received something, I had to share something in return, as it was customary to give and receive. So, sometimes when I saw snacks that Model liked, I would remember them and buy them as a gift.

One day, I asked Model why he liked models so much. He said that creating something was incredibly enjoyable for him. His dream was to become an inventor.

I found that really cool. He had a genuine dream, while at that time, I had never even thought about what my dream might be. Compared to me, Model seemed to have a clear goal. He had a sincere passion for a dream that I didn't have at the time.

When Model said he wanted to become an inventor, I responded.

"Amazing." I told Model that his dream was impressive, but I couldn't muster much enthusiasm.

Seeing him with a dream made me want to dream too. However,

I wasn't in a situation where I could afford to dream freely. I was doing the same tasks every day. I always had homework to do and had to prepare for school exams. That's how I could get into a good college. So, seeing Model, who was dreaming, made me a bit sad. Because of that, I couldn't tell him how amazing he was, even though I wanted to.

But my lackluster reaction seemed to make Model think that I was ignoring his dream. He said, "Do you actually think it's a mediocre dream?"

Model thought I was giving an insincere response. I wanted to let him know that I was sincere.

"It's not just words," I said. I paused for a moment, thinking about what else to say and continued.

"I don't have a dream like that. So, I hope your dream comes true."

Model seemed quite surprised. He didn't say anything.

Somehow, it felt like his dream would come true. If the day comes, I'd like to meet Model, my old friend, once again.

To me, Model was a special person. Since we spent a year together, he couldn't help but be special. But there were other people in our school. In our class alone, there were 30 students, so it was only natural.

The unfortunate thing was that not all of them liked me. And even more unfortunate was the fact that among those who didn't like me, there were some intimidating students, almost like bullies. No matter how the grade or class changed, there were always bullies.

One day, I was going about my school life as usual. But suddenly, one of the bullies called me out.

Most of the time, call from a bully wasn't a good sign. Spending time with them sometimes left me with bruises all over my body. Still, one of the bullies called me out, just like any other time. He called me out because he wanted to mess with me, as usual.

That day happened to be a "coming-of-age ceremony." I was chosen as the sacrifice for that coming-of-age ceremony.

As I mentioned before, the bullies were mainly made up of kids who matured early. People had to be pretty strong to join their organization. They had to be strong enough that others would be afraid of them.

However, not all early bloomers hung out with the bullies. In fact, the big kid who stole my homework was an early bloomer and had both size and strength. But he didn't associate with the bullies.

And not everyone who hung out with the bullies acted like a bully. They just happened to have similar builds, so it was easier for them to hang out with the bullies.

But the bullies hoped that the people they associated with would become the kind of people who could torment others. They wanted people to be afraid of them. I thought that I would be sad if others were afraid of me. Why did they want others to be afraid of them? It seemed like they couldn't face the others, if they weren't afraid of them. Somehow, I felt like the bullies were the ones who were the most scared.

Anyway, the bullies with bad intentions wanted to turn people who didn't usually act out into "bad people." That's what the coming-of-age ceremony was for.

The coming-of-age ceremony wasn't a big deal. They just brought one unpopular person. Then, they forced someone to beat him up, turning someone who didn't usually torment others into an official tormentor. The reason for beating him up wasn't that important. Sometimes they did it for no reason at all. The important thing was that after being beaten up, someone who wasn't usually malicious officially became malicious.

This time, I was chosen as the sacrificial lamb of that glorious coming-of-age ceremony.

On the day of the coming-of-age ceremony, I can't even remember how I was chosen as a sacrifice to the bullies. It was just an ordinary day. I had nothing special going on. The only moment I can recall is when one of the bullies called me into the restroom. At that time, I was dragged into the restroom without knowing what was happening. I couldn't even remember what I did wrong. I was just summoned by the bullies and suddenly found myself facing someone who was participating in the coming-of-age ceremony. If I had a little more memory left, I could explain it better. All I can say is that I woke up to find myself participating in the coming-of-age ceremony.

The coming-of-age ceremony took place in the school restroom, starting during a regular break time.

There were a total of four of us participating in the coming-of-age ceremony. The child who was brought to the ceremony as a potential tormentor, me, who became the sacrificial offering, and two others guarding the door.

At that time, the child who was brought to the coming-of-age ceremony was not a bully; he was more like a trainee. He was one of those trainees that the bullies were trying to groom into becoming bullies. The bullies were the two individuals guarding the door. They were the ones who brought the trainee and me to the coming-of-age ceremony.

The trainee wasn't typically hostile towards me; he was just physically imposing, but he had never done anything bad to me. So, the situation felt incredibly awkward to me at the time. In fact, he leaned more towards being kind because occasionally, when the bullies tried to harass me, he would step in to stop them. He would tell them to leave me alone. So, when I was with him, I didn't feel uncomfortable at all.

However, the bullies didn't appreciate the trainee's attitude, and that's why they brought him to the coming-of-age ceremony and were trying to force him to do bad things.

But the trainee seemed uncomfortable in the situation facing me as well. It seemed like he wasn't comfortable with the oppressive atmosphere that we both found ourselves in. Still, there were people making both me and the trainee even more uncomfortable—the two bullies guarding the door. They were the ones monitoring me to ensure I couldn't escape. Ironically, they were also keeping an eye on the trainee who had been associating with them. They wanted to make sure that he attacked me for real.

These bullies were blocking the entrance to the restroom, but they didn't say a word. They just stared at me and the trainee. They were like gatekeepers. There were two of them, one standing on the right side of the restroom door and the other on the left. They didn't physically block the way, but it didn't seem like they would let us leave if we tried to.

The gatekeepers didn't utter a word throughout the entire coming-of-age ceremony. However, the way they looked at us was incredibly intimidating. I couldn't understand why they were staring at the trainee so aggressively. The gatekeepers and the trainee used to hang out together regularly. I used to think that if people spent time together, they were friends. But looking at the way the gatekeepers were eyeing him made me realize that spending time together didn't necessarily mean they were friends. Friends were supposed to watch out for each other. However, the doorkeepers, who were bullies, didn't seem to be protecting the trainee. Were they not friends? Or had I misunderstood what friendship meant?

Still, I couldn't mock their friendship. I remembered the moment when I couldn't choose to help manga girl. Maybe I wasn't her friend either.

The coming-of-age ceremony was a trial for the trainee. If

the trainee didn't attack me, the doorkeepers would no longer consider him part of their group.

Being ousted from the bullies' group, while still not in their good books, would have spelled a bleak future for the trainee. He could have ended up just like me, someone who could be beaten up anytime. The bullies didn't like people who went against them.

I understood how the person being forced to make such a choice felt. I had felt it too on the day when the manga girl jumped. I was given a choice: save her and face the consequences or pretend not to know while she suffered. I chose to save myself.

I was the coward who pretended not to notice when the manga girl was in distress. So, perhaps I deserved whatever punishment was coming. The trainee had no reason to feel guilty if he hit me. Even if the trainee were to strike me, I could understand him. I had seen the conflict in him. He seemed to be trying not to hurt me, at least. So, I had no intention of blaming him even if he hit me. I just hoped to minimize the damage and let the day pass as uneventfully as possible.

At first, the trainee didn't touch me, so time was passing slowly. Then, one of the doorkeepers spoke up.

"Aren't you going to hit him?"

Hearing those words made me nervous. The moment I dreaded had finally arrived. Strangely, the trainee appeared even more bewildered. He was the one who was scared. What could have possibly frightened him?

Eventually, the trainee swung a punch at my arm, showing some restraint in his force.

But it seemed that the doorkeepers didn't like that at all.

"Was that a hit to you?" they said.

The trainee's expression grew even more fearful. Soon, he had made up his mind. He started to glare at me with a fierce look in his eyes. At that moment, I, too, felt fear from the trainee for the first time.

"I'm so dead," I thought to myself. I was calculating where and how I should be hit. With enough experience, I learned how to get hit while minimizing the pain. Typically, it was best to focus on getting hit in areas that could absorb the impact without hurting too much. For example, the arm was one of the least painful areas to be hit. Especially if I twisted my body at the moment of impact, I could send the shock away, making it relatively less painful. It was a skill I had developed over a long time.

The worst areas to get hit were the abdomen or the side, because they left lasting discomfort. So, if I were about to be hit in the abdomen or the side, I had to twist my body slightly. That way, the punch would land on my arm instead. Arms usually didn't hurt for long, so it was better to get hit there.

When it came to getting punched, besides minimizing the pain, there was another crucial factor: acting. The bullies typically didn't attack victims for any specific wrongdoing; they did it out of boredom. So, when they tried to harass me, I had to play along with their game. For example, right after getting punched, I had to fall as if collapsing. I also had to heave as if catching my breath. Adding a coughing sound effect was important too; it could give the bullies a sense of accomplishment. When they thought they had inflicted a lot of pain on me, they often stopped the violence. So, I put on an acting performance akin to a Hollywood actor.

Once again, it was time to showcase my well-honed skill of "getting hit with as little pain as possible." The trainee decided to turn me into a squashed dumpling. I prepared myself to fall adequately and positioned my arm to take the punch while preserving my bones.

Soon, the trainee was about to swing a punch. I tightly closed my eyes and slightly hunched my body. If I didn't hunch, my entire body would absorb the impact, making it hurt more. I was now mentally prepared.

However, I didn't hear the sound of the punch landing on my body. Instead, an unexpected voice came from outside the restroom where the coming-of-age ceremony was taking place.

"Is there someone inside?"

It was none other than the music teacher's voice. The music teacher was a truly intimidating person at school. Occasionally, I even referred to her in my mind as the "evil aunt." I got scolded by her every time during music class.

I was someone with absolutely no talent for playing musical instruments. Yet, the music teacher insisted on having me practice playing instruments every time. The problem was that instrument performance contributed to the final grade. I didn't even want to become a musician during the time. I couldn't understand why I had to learn them. But I couldn't argue with the teacher who was so pushy. What power did a student have?

It was the same voice as usual, when I heard the music teacher's voice coming from outside of the restroom. Still, there was no sweeter voice.

As soon as the music teacher's voice reached our ears, both the trainee and I froze. The doorkeepers were no exception. Their intimidating gazes vanished into thin air. All of a sudden, they wore the same puzzled expressions as regular students. It seemed that despite their usual tough act, they were just ordinary students at heart.

However, when I heard the voice, instead of relief, I felt a sense of curiosity. That's because the music teacher had no reason to be in the restroom.

In the middle school I attended, there were separate restrooms for teachers. The place where I was supposed to get hit wasn't meant for teachers. The bullies always avoided areas where they might encounter teachers. But such doubts didn't matter much at the moment. What was important was that I felt reasonably safe for the time being.

For a brief moment, the doorkeepers, the trainee, and I all just stared at each other. It was a moment when none of us knew what to do.

The doorkeepers were looking at me with astonished eyes.

"What should we do?" The expression on their faces seemed to be asking me a question.

I wanted to respond with, "How would I know?" I had been busy preparing myself to get hit with as little pain as possible. Demanding a solution to the current situation from me seemed unfair. Such a demand felt like a breach of contract. All I had to do was get hit, but they were asking for more than that.

However, such foolish worries were instantly halted by the music teacher.

"Open this door right now!"

The music teacher's voice was so loud that she could have been an opera singer. Not just anyone could teach music after all.

The doorkeepers immediately opened the door. The music teacher walked in, and for a moment, she looked around. Her expression contorted when she saw me trembling in fear.

"You, go back to your class."

The music teacher pointed at me and said. At that moment, I became an obedient student. I regretted ever thinking of the music teacher as an evil aunt. She seemed just as generous as she looked.

As I left the restroom, I could see the doorkeepers and the trainee following the music teacher. It seemed like I no longer had to worry.

I began walking back to my classroom. I was still filled with tension. I worried that I might face retaliation from the bullies later.

But I didn't care about what was going to happen to me in the future. I had a puzzling question that never left my head.

'How did the music teacher know to come here?'

I wasn't sure if I could get a clear answer for it.

Then, my friend, Model, approached me.

"Is everything okay?"

I was still tense, so I gave a simple reply.

"Yeah."

I nodded my head. I didn't really know if I was in a situation where everything was okay. I was just feeling dazed.

"I called the music teacher." Model said. I realized how the music teacher came to the restroom to save me.

"Oh, thanks."

I replied briefly.

I should have expressed my gratitude more accurately at the time. Still, my mind was so clouded that I couldn't pay attention to those details.

Model and I were close friends. We often played pranks together. Thus, I felt bitter to show him my pitiful state. Therefore, I pretended to be nonchalant.

But I couldn't forget that Model had called the music teacher.

'Model helped me,' I thought as the idea lingered in my mind throughout my return to the classroom.

A few days after Model called the music teacher to rescue me, I had the chance to meet with the trainee at my house. The recent incidents involving the manga girl and glasses girl had turned the school upside down. As a result, the school had taken extraordinary measures, including summoning all the parents to discuss the incidents and take actions according to their opinions. In simpler terms, they decided to follow my opinion when it came to disciplining the trainee. So, the trainee came to our house. He came urgently to apologize, hoping that I would forgive him.

Honestly, I wasn't really angry with the trainee. I had a unique temperament when it came to my emotions. I wasn't the type of person who held onto hurts. Even if something sad happened, I would forget it the next day. Holding onto negative memories felt like a disadvantage to me.

By the time the trainee came to see me, I had almost forgotten what had happened in the restroom. I didn't hold a grudge against him. He had tried his best not to hit me. So, when he apologized, I told him that it was okay. I didn't really care.

Of course, I didn't immediately forgive him from the beginning. This was partly because my mother was really angry. I tried to be accurate and determine who was in the wrong. My mother wasn't able to calm down easily.

But the trainee didn't come to our house alone. His parents were with him. And it was none other than the trainee's parents who apologized to me first.

To be honest, I was a bit weak when it came to adults. Especially when I saw scenes where adults would bow their heads, it made me very uncomfortable. I was still young. I didn't want to make adults bow their heads because of me.

When the trainee's parents apologized, my mother tried to stop them. It was clear to me that my mother didn't want to make others miserable. Seeing his own parents apologize, the trainee immediately bowed his head and apologized to me.

I scratched my head and told them that there wasn't really a problem. I was perfectly fine. Honestly, there were moments when that kid didn't even seem to want to hit me. The ones who had made my life difficult were actually the gatekeepers. They were the bullies who were guarding the exit of the restroom. Ironically, they didn't even come to apologize. They caused the trouble but seemed to escape any consequences.

I submitted my opinion to the school, stating that I was handling the situation with the trainee student just fine. I obtained a promise from the school that they would prevent any recurrence of such incidents. Finally, I made it clear that I didn't want any punishment for the trainee student.

The next day at school, when I met the trainee student, he called me to his spot and shouted loudly enough for everyone in the class to hear, "Anyone who messes with Hoon messes with me!"

The trainee was quite an amusing character. I hadn't even asked him to make such a statement. Still, from that point on, my school life became very stable. Whenever someone tried to bother me, the trainee student would ask, "Are you messing with Hoon?" No one dared to bother me then, even some bullies who occasionally tried. It was strange that they didn't touch me, as they were usually up to no good.

The trainee was quite clever. He knew that confronting those bullies could lead to fights, but he never backed down. He had an attitude of, "If they want to fight, let's fight." I thought fights might break out easily, but strangely, the bullies did nothing when the trainee student challenged them.

Thanks to him, I could enjoy a peaceful middle school life. With no one bothering me, I was genuinely happy going to school. Of course, studying for exams and completing assignments were still challenging. However, I didn't have to worry about other issues bothering me.

My life in South Korea, the southern part of Korea after it was divided into two parts, seemed to be getting better. But during the year of the coming-of-age ceremony, an incident occurred that made my parents reconsider. They were no longer sure about educating me in South Korea. They recommended that I study abroad.

I agreed. That's how my life in the United States began.

I had originally planned to study abroad right after the coming-of-age ceremony. After the coming-of-age ceremony, the incidents involving the manga girl and glasses girl became prominent again. Thanks to that, my parents became aware of how dangerous things were at school. Our family lost trust in the school.

However, during the process, my father advised me to at least graduate from middle school. This was because, in South Korea, people who graduated from the same school often met up. Even if we weren't friends at the time, we could become friends later. It was the beauty of time and relationship.

Graduating from middle school wasn't a difficult task. There wasn't much time left from the coming-of-age ceremony to the graduation ceremony. Thanks to that, I was able to graduate from middle school without any issues, with the trainee providing a lot of help.

I felt unexpectedly happy after the graduation ceremony. I didn't have many worries during the middle school graduation ceremony. I had experienced a lot of bullying at school, so I was concerned about the possibility of bullying being exposed during the graduation ceremony. My parents were there for the graduation ceremony. If I were to be bullied by the bullies in front of my parents, how much would it hurt their feelings?

I used to worry about that in the past. However, I no longer needed to worry about such things. Thankfully, nothing bad happened after the coming-of-age ceremony. Graduating without any concerns was a great relief.

After the graduation ceremony, I wanted to treat Model to a

meal. My mother gave me some pocket money, saying it was for buying delicious food for my friends. At that time, I only had one friend, Model. The intention behind the money was to have one last meal with a close friend before leaving for the United States. She gave me around $20, which was a substantial amount for me at the time. I had never received more than $7 for lunch expenses before.

However, surprisingly, the last meal with my friend before going to the United States almost ended on a sour note. The reason was that I thought the pocket money my mother gave me was too much. I decided to dine at an expensive restaurant. I believed $20 were enough to afford any kind of meal.

While walking around a shopping center with Model, I explored restaurants that seemed to serve delicious food. That's when I found a Japanese restaurant. It was elegantly decorated from the entrance.

I hadn't dined at such a restaurant before, but that day, I wanted to have a meal at a place like that. It was my last meal with a friend in South Korea. I didn't know how much it would cost. Still, I assumed that the pocket money my parents gave me would be enough.

But when I looked at the menu after sitting down, I was quite surprised. Even if I used up all my pocket money, I couldn't afford the cheapest dish for one person.

I had to awkwardly tell Model that it seemed like we should leave. Actually, Model had sensed from the beginning that the restaurant might be too expensive. He wanted to say something from the moment we entered the restaurant, probably realizing how expensive Japanese restaurants could be.

As we were about to get up from our seats, a waiter suddenly approached us and asked what was wrong. I honestly explained the situation. I told him that I had intended to treat my friend to something delicious before going abroad, but I didn't have enough money. So, I apologized and said we were leaving.

However, the waiter went to the owner and said something. The owner gave some instructions, and the waiter returned to us shortly afterward.

The waiter asked us how much money we had. I told her I had about $20. Initially, it felt like a significant amount, almost too heavy to carry around. $20 was quite a lot of pocket money for kids.

The waiter said she would prepare a meal based on the money I had. I explained that I couldn't even afford the cheapest dish. However, she told me not to worry and asked us to stay.

Model and I just sat there without thinking too much. Soon, she brought out some corn cheese. Model and I enjoyed the corn cheese. In fact, the portion of corn cheese was quite generous, and there were many side dishes. The table was filled with food.

I thought the corn cheese costed about $20. So, I assumed the restaurant owner had prepared about $20 worth of corn cheese. Nevertheless, I was incredibly satisfied. The corn cheese was delicious. It felt like a good dish to eat in celebration before parting ways with a friend.

But before we could finish the corn cheese, a salad was served. I didn't know why another dish was being served. I thought maybe the salad was an additional side dish. I just thought the restaurant's service was exceptionally good.

However, before we could finish the salad, a grilled fish dish arrived. It was a long, slender fish. I didn't understand why another dish was being served. It was after I had already eaten the corn cheese and salad. So, I thought the grilled fish was surprisingly inexpensive. I thought it was part of the treat by the owner.

The grilled fish was delicious. I usually didn't enjoy eating fish, especially dealing with bones. But this grilled fish was easy to eat, bones and all. Thanks to that, I got to try a new dish I hadn't known about before.

However, before we could finish eating the grilled fish, a stew was served. Eventually, Model and I were too full to finish the stew. We couldn't eat it all. I had no idea if I could cover the cost of all these dishes with $20. I even started to think that $20 might be a lot of money if it could pay for all these dishes.

After we finished eating all the food, Model and I got up from our seats and headed to the cashier. However, I was worried. No matter how I looked at it, I didn't think $20 would be enough to pay for all the food. I had eaten, and Model had joined me for the meal. So, I thought maybe I'd need more money than just $20.

Model seemed to have similar thoughts and put out all the money he had. He had about $8. So, together, we had a total of $28. We put all the money we had on the counter at the cashier. If that wasn't enough to cover the cost of the food, we would have to apologize and explain that it was all we had. Otherwise, I had to call my parents to pay for the meal.

However, at the cashier's counter told us we didn't need to pay. I couldn't understand what she meant. I was sure we had eaten our meal, but she said we didn't need to pay.

"Was there a situation where I didn't have to pay for the meal?" That thought crossed my mind. I thought there might have been occasions that I didn't know because I was young. I even considered the possibility that Model might have paid for the meal when I wasn't aware. However, he also had no idea how the meal had been paid for. Moreover, we walked out of the restaurant with the $28 we had initially, not having paid a single cent for the meal.

At that time, as young as I and Model were, we didn't think much of it. We just considered ourselves fortunate that the meal cost had been taken care of somehow. We thought of it as a magical, unexplained event that had happened to us. We felt incredibly lucky.

However, as I grew older, I came to understand what had happened. The waitress and the owner of that Japanese restaurant were truly kind-hearted people. They had hoped that my friend and I could enjoy a nice meal together before I went abroad, even if we didn't have enough money. So, despite the shortage of money, they treated us to an exquisite Japanese course meal. Thanks to them, I could leave for the United States with a happy memory of a last wonderful meal. I felt really grateful for that.

When I grew up, I wanted to become an adult like the waitress and the owner of that Japanese restaurant. Somehow, I felt that if I could become that kind of person, they would be pleased. Someday, if I had the opportunity, I wanted to meet them again and express my gratitude.

CHAPTER 5

● ● ● ● ●

After the meal at the Japanese restaurant, I didn't stay in South Korea for long and soon departed for the United States. When I first arrived in the U.S., it didn't feel real. Being separated from my family was something I couldn't fully grasp at the time. Studying abroad meant I had to navigate life on my own and adapt to a new culture. Still, I had never been alone.

The idea of being apart from my family was unsettling, especially at the airport. When I went to the airport to get on a plane to the United States, I was with my family. We were together even until I got my tickets.

However, things changed when I reached security checkpoints. Airports had security checkpoints, where I had to have my belongings inspected before boarding the plane. Items like lighters, liquids, or weapons were not allowed on the aircraft.

Still, because someone could try to bring them on the aircraft, security personnel checked the luggage of passengers.

Before reaching the security checkpoint, there were immigration officers checking passports. Up until that point, I was still with some of my family members. We had traveled to the airport together; my parents and I were there, although my siblings weren't present. My younger brother wanted to play games. So he stayed at home. I couldn't blame him since I would have done the same if he were leaving.

Anyway, when I presented my passport to the immigration officer, my parents didn't show their passports. I showed mine and proceeded towards the security checkpoint. This was the moment when I separated from my parents. As I continued towards the security checkpoint, my parents didn't follow.

The situation felt awkward. I was used to always being with my family wherever we went. It felt strange that they weren't coming with me. Despite having only one ticket for the flight, it felt like my family should have been coming along.

Throughout my journey to the security checkpoint, I kept looking back, expecting my parents to follow. However, they didn't. They simply waved and stayed where they were. I didn't have any significant thoughts at that moment, except wondering if I was truly leaving alone.

Once I passed through the security checkpoint, my parents were no longer visible. I hesitated for a moment, feeling like something might be wrong. It was as if I had been walking my dog. My dog stopped and waited for me if my family didn't keep moving. However, there was one crucial difference: the dog would eventually catch up with other family members, but my parents didn't.

So, I continued my journey to study abroad, suddenly realizing that I had arrived in the United States without my family.

When I first arrived in the United States, there was only one thought on my mind:

"What do I do now?"

I had no idea what to do at the airport. All I knew was the name of the school I was supposed to attend. However, I didn't know how to get to that school. I didn't know if there were buses or subways near the airport. I had no idea about the fares. Moreover, I couldn't speak English, so I couldn't even ask for directions. I had really come to the U.S. with absolutely no preparation.

The only advice my parents had given me before leaving was:

"When you arrive, meet the dormitory host who will find you and do exactly as he says."

The dormitory host was the resident advisor at the dormitory I would be staying in. Thankfully, he had come to pick me up at the airport in the United States. He was waiting at the airport with a large sign bearing my name. So, as soon as I completed the immigration process and exited the airport, I could see him waiting for me.

At that time, I had just arrived from South Korea. My phone didn't work in the United States. South Korean mobile phone services didn't apply in the U.S. So, if I hadn't met the dormitory host at the airport, I would have been lost.

The dormitory host drove me in his car towards the school. I wasn't even sure if this person was really the dormitory host; he just seemed like a kind person, so I followed along. If he hadn't been the dormitory host and had turned out to be a kidnapper, I might not be writing this story now.

Fortunately, the dormitory host was not a kidnapper. He soon brought me to the school. It was a beautiful school with a large lake in the center.

At the school entrance, the dormitory host stopped at the security office and explained the reason for our visit to the security guard. He told the guard that he had brought a new international student.

"Welcome to America," the security guard said to me. It sounded like a very nice phrase, but at the time, I didn't understand it well. My English wasn't proficient yet.

The school I arrived at was quite large, unlike my middle school. What set it apart was the spacious campus with various buildings scattered around. In contrast, my middle school back in South Korea only had the school building and a sports field. My American high school, on the other hand, had a central lake, a separate parking lot, and even two sports fields. Going around the school once would make me break a sweat due to its vast size. The rumor that land prices were cheaper in America than South Korea was true.

The dormitory host took me to a building located at the far back of the school. On the way to the back, I passed several other buildings, but the one at the very back was the best. It was going to be my dormitory. I was delighted to have the opportunity to stay in such a nice building.

The dormitory had a variety of delicious snacks. The dormitory supervisor had even stocked up on Korean foods like ramen or seaweed for me. To be honest, there wasn't any food that I didn't like. Especially among Korean foods, there was nothing I disliked, so I could enjoy any snack I wanted. When I was in Korea, my parents restricted me from eating snacks, but in the dormitory, there was no one to stop me. In the United States, no one scolded me for eating. I could eat two packets of ramen at once, and no one would say a word. In South Korea, people used to nag me every time I ate, telling me that I would gain weight. Thanks to that, I turned into a hamster stuffed with almonds in

WARREN BUFFETT AND THE STREET CLEANER

the United States. I could eat almonds from a bowl as much as I wanted, and I ended up gaining weight like a bear preparing for hibernation. My belly stuck out like a winter-ready bear.

The beginning in the United States was much happier than I had expected. I forgot to call my parents back in South Korea; I was so caught up in enjoying my new life. After a few days, my parents were the ones who called me first. As soon as they called, they asked me why I hadn't called them. They wondered if I didn't miss my family. However, their prediction was not entirely inaccurate. I was enjoying life in the United States so much that I had forgotten to contact them.

I told them the truth. As a result, my parents lamented that they had spent so much money on sending an ungrateful child like me overseas. I regretted telling the truth. Sometimes, it's not necessary to always tell the truth.

But my happiness didn't last long. It wasn't long before the school year started. I had to transition from being a free person to a student once again. Moreover, this time, I was becoming a high school student. I could sense that more challenging times lay ahead than when I was in middle school.

Before going to school, I had one worry. I was concerned that I might experience bullying in the United States as well. Throughout my school years in South Korea, I had been the victim of bullying. There was no guarantee that I wouldn't be bullied in the United States. Americans were people too. I had a feeling they might not like me just like some South Koreans didn't. I was still struggling with understanding English. I was placed in a situation where I didn't know how to navigate. However, I didn't need to find the solution myself. Thankfully, in the United States, I was able to get along well with people.

The first class I attended in the United States was a history class, which happened to be the subject I found most challenging even back in South Korea. I used to receive disappointing scores on history exams in South Korea. School grades could be quite emotional. But now, in this new environment called the United States, I was starting with the most difficult subject. Somehow, I had a feeling that many ominous things might happen in the United States.

However, all those worries vanished the moment I walked through the door to start my history class. I was startled by the cheers and shouts of excitement coming from inside. My American classmates welcomed me with enthusiasm. The applause seemed never-ending. I even thought that maybe the United States had won the World Cup.

As I entered the classroom, the history teacher extended his hand to shake mine, welcoming me warmly. He was a young and kind-looking teacher with a neatly groomed beard. His beard was quite impressive. It gave me a sense of reassurance. I felt like he would take good care of me. Americans indeed seemed to look great with beards; the rumors were true.

The warm welcome from my history teacher and classmates made me forget all my worries. If not for their kindness, I wouldn't have been able to explain the sense of relief I felt at that moment.

However, there was one day when my history teacher shaved his beard. I could never forget the shock I experienced that day. He looked like someone who had killed five people that morning. Seeing my history teacher without his beard made him quite intimidating. It was as if babies witnessing their dad shaving for the first time and crying because they didn't recognize him. Maybe the feeling of relief I felt during my first class had something to do with my history teacher's beard after all.

Fortunately, life in the United States was quite peaceful. There were some challenges, but I was able to overcome them.

My first challenge began with the history class I took from the very beginning. It was related to my friendships.

Fortunately, I wasn't subjected to bullying, but unfortunately, I unintentionally upset someone.

The first friend I approached in the United States was the one who sat on my left in the history class. I greeted him with the only word I knew at the time: "Hello." Thankfully, I knew how to say "hello," which was an easy word to remember, having seen it countless times in movies. However, I couldn't engage in any other conversation because I didn't know English well. I felt regretful that I couldn't offer better greetings to the friends who welcomed me.

Despite the language barrier, I made an effort to connect with my classmates. I started by greeting everyone individually with a simple "hello." However, I realized it would be nice to know their names, as addressing them by name would create a friendlier atmosphere. So, I decided to learn their names, starting with the friend on my right, who had warmly welcomed me. I asked him for his name, and he told me it was Brandon.

Brandon was a very cheerful friend. He was the one who contributed most to the lively atmosphere in our classroom. I felt that we could become good friends. Brandon was exceptionally kind to me, making me feel happy about having a new friend in the United States. It gave me the impression that I might be able to make many friends in America.

I decided to learn the names of my other classmates as well, starting with a friend nearby.

I asked my friend on the left for his name. He told me his name was Holden. I greeted Holden and said it was nice to meet him.

However, suddenly Brandon called me and whispered something to me. "The friend next to you is not Holden; his name is douchebag. You should call him douchebag. Try calling him douchebag."

I had thought my friend on the left was Holden, but Brandon, using simple words that I could understand, told me that my friend on the left's name was douchebag. I felt like I had made a big mistake, and I almost called my friend on the left the wrong name. So, as a way of apologizing, I spoke to my friend on the left.

"Hello, Douchebag."

But suddenly, my friend on the left began to ignore my greetings. He had been smiling and saying hello to me just a moment ago, but now he seemed angry for some reason.

I felt like I had encountered the racial barrier that I had only heard about before. Experiencing racial discrimination was painful.

The moment I felt that barrier, I felt a sense of responsibility. That responsibility was to break down the racial barrier. I believed that love could transcend discrimination. After all, love conquers all.

Every time I met my friend on the left in class, I greeted him using the name 'douchebag' that Brandon had told me. At first, it was not easy to gauge his reaction. My friend on the left ignored me every day. Nevertheless, with a heart full of love and patience, I continued to greet him by calling his name. Eventually, he started talking to me too. Love triumphed.

However, the first words my friend on the left spoke to me were strange.

"My name is not douchebag; it's Holden," my friend on the left suddenly said. I was confused because I had thought his name was 'douchebag'. So, I asked Brandon to confirm his name once again. Brandon had been very helpful to me, and I trusted him.

Brandon insisted that his name was indeed 'douchebag'. He told me to trust him. I didn't want to doubt my friend, but as time passed, and my English improved, I began to realize the issue.

It turned out that my friend on the left was indeed named Holden. Brandon had given me the wrong name. The problem was that the word 'douchebag' that Brandon had told me to use was a derogatory term used to make fun of someone. So, every time I called Holden by that name, it hurt his feelings. That's why he had been ignoring my greetings. I had mistakenly thought it was because Holden didn't like me.

Once I realized my mistake, I apologized to Holden and tried to greet him correctly. Over time, we became friends. I was relieved. I had almost missed out on having a good friend like Holden.

Friends like Holden and Brandon helped me adapt to life in the United States. I also learned some interesting slang terms. My life in the United States was far from boring from the very beginning.

I could live with a smile in the United States. I was enjoying my life there in my own way. However, the biggest source of laughter for me was my grades. They were so abysmal that all I could do was to laugh. I was getting straight zeros in all my subjects. If I had sent a dog to school in my place, it might have performed better.

Life in the United States wasn't easy at first. First, I couldn't speak English at all. It took me a long time even to learn people's names. But there was a more significant problem than not knowing English – I knew nothing about the United States.

Even the history class I first took was no walk in the park. I had to take tests. I was supposed to write down all the states in the United States. Honestly, I couldn't even remember all 5 states in South Korea. (Was it 5?) How could I possibly memorize 50 states in the United States? (Was it 50?)

Nevertheless, strangely, I didn't feel any problems during my early days in the United States. Getting zero scores had almost become a hobby for me. But there was nothing particularly special about why my mind was so peaceful. I didn't even know I was getting zero scores.

My first English teacher was Mrs. Cornell, an elderly lady with a head full of white hair. I took English class with Brandon. In the class, he always made me laugh. Brandon's pranks in the class were always beyond imagination. Brandon strangely never used the classroom door; instead, he entered through the window every time. Mrs. Cornell would repeatedly tell him not to do it, but Brandon just didn't listen. Honestly, I couldn't defend Brandon when I thought of Mrs. Cornell. His pranks sometimes went too far. But, to be honest, Brandon was hilarious. Even the way he breathed was funny. There was never a dull moment when I was around him.

Mrs. Cornell was a kind lady, but she was of a certain age. Maybe that's why she wasn't very tech-savvy. Once, Brandon brought a wireless mouse to the classroom. He secretly connected it to Mrs. Cornell's laptop. A wireless mouse is a small device that, when plugged into a laptop, allows a person to control it remotely. Mrs. Cornell seemed unaware of it.

During class, Mrs. Cornell would often use PowerPoint with her laptop for teaching. However, there were times when she turned away from the board, showing the screen with the PowerPoint, and faced the students. At those moments, Brandon would use the wireless mouse to turn off the PowerPoint. So, when Mrs. Cornell turned back to the screen, the PowerPoint was off.

The situation was just too funny, and I can't say I was a model student for laughing. But I couldn't help it; no one could. Even the so-called "good" students were hiding their laughter by burying their faces in their desks. Honestly, if Mrs. Cornell had been sitting among the students, she might have been laughing too.

Still, Mrs. Cornell was a wonderful teacher. Even when she found out later that it was Brandon's prank, she handled it with grace. If I were Mrs. Cornell, I would have had a hard time controlling my anger. It turned out that not just anyone can be a teacher.

Mrs. Cornell genuinely cared about her students. If a student needed help, she was always willing to assist. However, there was one troublesome student who made her uneasy, and that student was me. My bad habit got the best of Mrs. Cornell.

When I first came to the United States, I had a habit of nodding my head vigorously whenever I had a conversation with someone. The English I had learned in South Korea was a bit different from the English spoken in the United States. For example, "What's up" was one of the most common expressions used in the United States, almost like a greeting. However, I had never learned such expressions in South Korea.

In South Korea, I often learned expressions that were not commonly used in the United States. For example, there's the way I learned to introduce myself. Self-introduction was a big part of Korean education, and we were taught a very standardized way to do it. The expressions we learn are so ingrained that I still haven't forgotten them.

"Hello. Let me introduce myself. My name is Hoon Choi. I like to play soccer. Nice to meet you all." This kind of self-introduction was found in every textbook. I thought this was the only way to introduce myself in the U.S. However, living in the U.S., I realized that hardly anyone actually uses this formalized way of introducing themselves. Americans prefers a more casual and straightforward approach to self-introductions. For instance, saying something like "My name is Elizabeth. Just call me Ellie." is often all that's needed for a self-introduction. They simply stated their name and maybe how they'd like to be addressed. That's it. This was something I only truly grasped through direct communication with Americans.

As a result, it took time to adapt to American English, especially for those who weren't proficient in the language. At the beginning, I could barely communicate in English. It felt like even parrots mimicked English better than I did. When someone approached me in English, I couldn't respond effectively because

I didn't understand what they were saying.

I worried that my lack of understanding might come across as me ignoring what they were saying. This worry led to a habit of nodding my head emphatically during conversations. I did it not for any specific reason but to convey that I was paying attention, even if I didn't comprehend the words being spoken. It was my way of showing that I was engaged in the conversation. Over time, this nonverbal communication became a part of my conversational style.

The same phenomenon repeated itself in a conversation with Mrs. Cornell. It was a regular day when we were about to end our class. Mrs. Cornell called me over. She started saying something, but I couldn't understand anything. So, I kept nodding my head repeatedly. Consequently, Mrs. Cornell looked puzzled but eventually let me go.

After some time, Mrs. Cornell called me over again. This time she seemed more urgent in her explanation. However, to be honest, I still had no idea what she was saying. So, I nodded my head again, and Mrs. Cornell let me go once more.

A little while later, Mrs. Cornell called me again. I thought she must be concerned about something specific due to me being a Korean student. Otherwise, she wouldn't have called me so frequently.

However, it turned out that Mrs. Cornell wasn't calling me because she wanted to give me special attention. It was because if certain measures weren't taken, I might not graduate.

Mrs. Cornell explained something to me once more. I thought I should nod my head again. But this time, the conversation didn't end easily as it usually did when I just nodded my head. Mrs. Cornell kept talking as I continued nodding, and eventually, she stopped speaking. I thought the conversation was over and tried to leave the classroom, but for some reason, Mrs. Cornell stopped me from leaving and gestured for me to follow her to her computer.

She started searching for our school's name on Google. I was aware of our school's name and Google since I had visited our school's website before coming to this class. However, I was surprised to learn that there was another website related to our school that I had never known about. This new website was quite unique, as it required an ID and a password to access. Until then, I had never needed an ID and password to access our school's website.

I was just quietly observing Mrs. Cornell, trying to understand what she was doing. Then, she handed me the keyboard and pointed to the place where I needed to enter the ID and password.

I didn't know what she wanted me to do, so this time, I just stared at her in confusion. Since she didn't say anything this time, I could sense that she expected something from me. So, for the first time, I took a different action and pointed with my finger to the website while shaking my head side to side, indicating that I didn't know what to do.

"I don't know" was the limit of what I could say with my limited English skills. The reason was that I didn't know the ID and password. I didn't even know such a website existed, so how could I possibly know the ID and password?

Mrs. Cornell looked quite flustered. She furrowed her eyebrows and brought her hand to her chin. She seemed to be pondering what to do.

Eventually, Mrs. Cornell began typing something for the ID and password. I noticed that her ID was a combination of her name and some numbers, so I realized that she was logging in with her own account.

She started navigating through the site. I saw a familiar class name on the screen. It was the name of the English class I had been attending. I knew that class well, as I had been taking it.

Mrs. Cornell clicked on that class, and a list of students appeared. I had started to remember the names of some of the students by then, and I saw my name on the list.

Mrs. Cornell clicked on my name, and at that moment, a list appeared. There were some entries on it, but I didn't know what they represented. However, one strange thing was that at the end of each entry, there was always the number '0' and the letter 'F.'

I found this strange because it seemed like the website Mrs. Cornell showed me was a platform for managing student grades. The entries had some unappealing numbers and letters. '0' and 'F' were not good grades on a report card. Unless I didn't submit an assignment at all, I wouldn't normally receive a grade of 0 or an 'F.'

I couldn't believe that I might have received an 'F' or a 0 because I thought I had never missed an assignment in Mrs. Cornell's class. So, I decided to take my time and try to figure out what this website was about. However, the more I looked at it, the more it seemed like the website displayed my grades. I realized that the numbers on the site actually represented my grades.

It was a mind-blowing scene. I had never seen a report card with so many '0's and 'F's before. They looked like Morse code. When I put them together, it seemed to spell out, "My school life is ruined."

That's when I realized that something was terribly wrong. I had always thought that I was doing quite well in school up to that point. I had never seen a homework assignment. I had turned in a blank sheet for every test. Yet somehow, I thought I was doing well in school. I looked at Mrs. Cornell with a puzzled expression. I thought I had been doing all my assignments up to that point.

Mrs. Cornell clicked on one of the entries in the list, which happened to be one of my assignments. It showed '0' and 'F' on the part that she showed me.

I looked even more puzzled and couldn't understand why Mrs. Cornell had given me '0's and 'F's. Then, Mrs. Cornell pointed to a section that said 'Submission,' and there was 'none' written there. That's when I finally realized that I hadn't been doing my homework. I pointed at the list and said to Mrs. Cornell, "ahh... homework?" That was my own way of asking, "Is this homework?" I wasn't used to speaking in complete sentences at the time, so I had to convey my intentions with a single word. Fortunately, Mrs. Cornell was quick to catch on. She understood what I was trying to say with just that word. It was only then that Mrs. Cornell realized that I didn't know how to do homework.

Homework in American schools was quite different. I had to check and submit my homework online using a computer. When I was in South Korea, I had never checked or submitted my homework online. I always had to write things by hand. In addition, in South Korea, teachers would always tell us about the homework. Sometimes, they would even write it on the blackboard. I was used to that culture. So, I naturally assumed it would be the same in the U.S. I thought that if there was homework, the teachers would write it on the blackboard. However, there were no teachers writing homework on the blackboard in the U.S. Instead, they posted the assignments on a website that required the ID and password I mentioned earlier.

In the end, I had no idea whether there had been homework all along. I had complacently thought that I had been doing all my assignments. I was growing an "All F" report card in high school while Anna and Elsa from the movie Frozen were raising Olaf the snowman.

When I looked back, the fact that there was no homework seemed strange. I hadn't done any homework for the first three months. Most people would have wondered, "Why is there no homework?" But I thought, "In America, you don't have to do homework!" I had this idea that America was a dreamland without homework. I thought having no homework was kind of the American Dream.

However, America was still a place where people lived. Schools assigned homework, and students were expected to complete it. Someone once said that taxes and homework were inevitable, and that person must have been a genius.

So, I spent half of my first semester in the United States with straight zeros. Typically, a student who gets such poor grades for an entire semester would have a hard time getting into college. Colleges wanted students who had worked hard during high school.

However, I was incredibly lucky. This was because, when applying to colleges, I didn't have to submit my grades for 9th grade. Unlike South Korea, where high school was only three years, the United States had a four-year high school system. Students were considered high school students from 9th to 12th grade. Still, for some reason, in the United States, colleges only required grades from the last three years of high school. They only asked for grades from 10th to 12th grade. Thanks to that, I was able to get into the college I wanted. I was fortunate that the college I attended didn't ask for my 9th-grade grades. If the college had found out my 9th-grade grades, they might have revoked my diploma.

CHAPTER 6

• • • • • •

After going through that crisis, I started to focus more on my studies. My 9th-grade grades were nothing short of disastrous. It felt like there were nuclear bombs going off in each subject. My report card was the only one in the world that had survived so many nuclear explosions.

Studying was challenging. It was mentally taxing and physically demanding work. Still, I coped with the task well and had some benefit.

Moreover, I discovered a way to relieve stress, and that was through exercise. I started playing soccer. The school I attended had a soccer team. It was known for their exceptional skills. It had both a first-string and a second-string team. Our school's first-string soccer team had a reputation for being excellent. It even had a coach who recruited talented students.

I wasn't particularly good at soccer. I didn't make it onto the first-string team; in fact, I had only been playing soccer for less than a year. So, I ended up on the second-string team.

The first-string and second-string teams were entirely different. They didn't even compete in the same league. The first-string was like a professional team, while the second-string was more like an amateur team. Their training methods were also different. I had a chance to train with the first-string team once. It felt like I needed five hearts and five sets of lungs just to keep up. Maybe the first-string players were aliens. I knew America was hiding them.

Of course, the training for the second-string team wasn't easy either. It was some of the most intense training I had ever experienced. I did some grueling workouts. Once, I had to carry a teammate on our backs and run uphill continuously. I couldn't help but feel grateful to the inventor of the escalator after that. Running uphill was incredibly challenging.

Playing soccer brought many positive changes to my life. First, the rigorous training improved my fitness level significantly. I used to be a fat and unhealthy student. However, after I started to exercise, I became a fat and healthy student. (Training stimulated my appetite too much that I couldn't lose the weight.)

Additionally, soccer was a sport that helped me make new friends. Whenever I played soccer together, almost anyone can become my friend. Soccer teammates didn't really have an issue with my English skills. Honestly, soccer didn't require much English proficiency during games. If the opposing team put pressure on me during a game, all I needed to do was shout, "Man on!" When a player on my team had the ball, the opposing team would try to take it away. So, I had to alert the player with the ball that an opponent was closing in, hence the shout of "Man on!" During a game, it's not easy to notice someone approaching me secretly, so this communication was crucial.

Apart from that, I could simply shout "Hey!" to request a pass. As long as I could shout any word, my teammates could understand well enough to pass me the ball. Even shouting "Washington DC!" would have worked, although I was in Florida.

With just a few words, communication on the soccer field was entirely possible. Occasionally, when I wanted to swear at the opposing team, I did it in Korean. Swearing in English could get me a warning from the referees. Sometimes, when referees made questionable calls, I would swear at them in Korean. Strangely, the referees understood the Korean swears, so I had to be careful. If I messed up, I could get ejected from the game.

The dormitory supervisor didn't have a problem with me playing sports. In fact, they recommended that I exercise frequently. They didn't mind if I spent half of my day playing soccer. Thanks to that, I found a hobby that I could enjoy for a lifetime. Still, I eventually had to quit due to frequent knee injuries.

The dormitory supervisor did, however, request that I focus on my schoolwork and prepare for exams. If they thought I wasn't studying enough at school, they would express their concerns. Our school was responsible for the well-being of international students who had come to study abroad. They wanted us to grow up as responsible adults.

So, I had to dedicate two hours of study time every evening. During that time, I couldn't do anything else; it was a dormitory rule. This was known as "study time." I had to abide by it. I balanced this study time with my desire to exercise.

With this structured routine, I eventually became a junior. In the American educational system, a junior was an 11th-grade student. The junior year was when students typically started preparing for college admissions. However, I did have one concern. I hadn't really thought much about my future. I hadn't considered which college I wanted to attend or what I wanted to major in.

When I was in high school, apart from soccer, I didn't have many other interests. I played video games occasionally, but most of my time was dedicated to soccer. Improving my soccer skills a little more every day was the most rewarding thing for me.

However, my friends around me started to focus on college admissions. At that time, I was playing soccer so frequently that I had become close to the members of the first-string soccer team. They, too, were worried about college admissions.

Most of my soccer teammates aspired to attend prestigious universities known for their soccer programs and dreamed of becoming professional soccer players by the time they graduated from college. I admired them for having such clear goals. Seeing my friends getting serious about their college preparations, I decided to start researching universities in the United States. I didn't have much knowledge about universities, both in the United States and South Korea. I hadn't really cared about the college admissions process.

During this time, one of my friends advised me to visit the school's college counselor. Our school had professionals who specialized in helping students with college admissions, known as advisors. These advisors could provide guidance on the college application process and help students find suitable colleges and majors.

The advisor at our school was a tremendous help to me. She understood that I was new to the whole process of researching U.S. colleges and patiently guided me through it. She began by suggesting that I should decide on a major field of study. A major was a specific academic discipline in which I'll gain specialized knowledge during my college years. There were countless major options available, covering a wide range of academic fields.

The truth was, I didn't have a specific passion or calling for any particular field. Choosing a major was a daunting task for me. However, the advisor offered valuable advice. She recommended that I think about the subjects in which I had excelled in high school. The idea was to leverage my strengths and pursue a major that aligned with my existing skills.

At that time, I was performing well in subjects like math and science. I had already covered advanced math topics during my middle school years in South Korea, so high school math was relatively easy for me.

I told the advisor that my grades in math and science were decent. In response, she introduced me to an "Engineering College," a university specializing in engineering education. Engineering was a field of study that I hadn't explored during my high school years. I didn't know exactly what I would study in college or what engineering entailed, even now that I've graduated from an engineering program.

Fortunately, the advisor provided a brief explanation of what engineering colleges were about and shared some information about what was needed to apply to them.

To apply to engineering colleges, like most other universities, I needed to submit my high school transcript, SAT scores, letters of recommendation, and individual essays. There were some additional requirements specific to each university, but generally, these four factors played a significant role in determining admission.

At the time I was preparing for college admissions, I was near the end of my 11th grade. My past grades were fixed. I couldn't change them through effort. I had to submit the scores I had received earlier. So, my focus shifted to the SAT scores, letters of recommendation, and individual essays.

The SAT evaluated three main areas: reading, writing, and math skills. Honestly, I wasn't lacking in math skills. I consistently scored near perfect on math tests. Making just one or two mistakes was considered a bad day for me. Asians were generally strong in math, while Americans tended to excel in reading and writing.

Reading and writing were challenging areas for me. For me, good grades for reading and writing were like a pink dolphin in the Amazon. Some say that it existed, but I had no chance to see it. All the grades that I received were like an anglerfish. It was ugly. Well, the anglerfish at least tasted good, but my grades weren't even mouth-watering. If I had them, I had to have food poisoning.

Reading, in particular, was something I struggled with immensely. No matter how much I practiced, my reading scores just wouldn't improve. Even now, it's hard to believe that I'm writing a book, given how poor my reading skills were.

The SAT reading passages often featured people, history, or books I hadn't heard of before, but many of these texts were about remarkable individuals. Additionally, there were passages related to planets and natural phenomena. They often included complex explanations. I sometimes wondered if the world really needed to be so complicated.

What's funny was that no matter how much I studied, my scores didn't seem to improve much. In the past, I had read a traditional fairy tale called 'The Tortoise and the Hare.' It was a story about a race between a tortoise and a hare. The hare was much faster than the tortoise in terms of running speed. Normally, the hare couldn't lose in a running race against the tortoise. However, due to the hare's overconfidence, it took a nap during the race. As a result, the slow but steady tortoise ended up winning the race.

This story taught many valuable lessons, and the most important one was that consistent effort brings rewards. However, while studying for the SAT reading section, I discovered a flaw in this lesson. No matter how hard I tried, my SAT reading scores didn't improve. I needed to create a new fairy tale titled 'Hoon and the SAT.'

Still, in the end, my consistent effort led to an improvement in my SAT reading scores, which became sufficient for college applications. I guess I didn't need to write a new fairy tale.

Fortunately, writing scores also increased alongside reading scores, which was truly fortunate. I had a few colleges in mind that I wanted to apply to, and my scores exceeded their admission thresholds.

I also received recommendation letters from several teachers, which was also fortunate. I had a lot of teachers I really liked in high school. My initial history teacher and Mr. Cornell, of course, but also the physics and English teachers I met later on. They were not only excellent educators but also wonderful people in general.

In the end, I requested recommendation letters from Mr. Freeman, my physics teacher, and Mrs. Backfield, my English teacher, both of whom I really admired. Mr. Freeman was a genuinely fun teacher. He always brought props to his physics classes and demonstrated physical phenomena so that I could see them in action. He also told a lot of jokes, making his classes anything but dull.

However, there was a time when Mr. Freeman got really upset. It happened when we were watching the news together. One day, there was a live broadcast of a car chase where a vehicle was evading the police. The fleeing car was changing lanes recklessly and trying to escape from the police. Many students, including myself, found the video exciting to watch. The escaping car seemed almost supernatural in how it eluded the police. Some students were laughing and enjoying the show.

But when Mr. Freeman saw students laughing, he got really angry. It was the first time I had seen him so upset. He was usually a very kind and jovial person. However, after hearing his explanation, I realized that his anger was justified. Mr. Freeman pointed out that the actions of the fleeing car were extremely dangerous. In reality, the car was swerving between lanes and, at times, even driving against traffic. It was willing to do anything to escape from the police. However, such actions were extremely dangerous. It could have easily resulted in accidents with other cars, or worse, pedestrians being hit. Mr. Freeman was a physics teacher. He had a good understanding of what could happen when a car hit a person. So, Mr. Freeman got upset because he wanted to instill the concept of safety in students and make sure they didn't laugh when witnessing dangerous driving. After hearing the reasons behind Mr. Freeman's anger, I decided to ask him for a recommendation letter. He had proven himself to be an excellent educator in my eyes.

The other teacher who provided me with a recommendation letter was Mrs. Backfield. She had been a professor at a nearby Florida university before coming to our high school.

Initially, I wasn't particularly fond of Mrs. Backfield. Her classes were quite challenging. She taught English, which was one of my weakest subjects. However, there was a turning point that made me really appreciate Mrs. Backfield. It happened during a midterm assignment.

Interestingly, Mrs. Backfield's class required submitting essays instead of taking traditional exams for midterms. We had to read certain texts and then write extensive essays. I felt overwhelmed by the idea of writing such lengthy essays at first. Writing was a task that I found extremely difficult.

I decided to be honest with Mrs. Backfield about my struggles. I told her that writing lengthy essays felt like a tremendous burden to me. There was not even ChatGPT that would do the assignment back then. (Of course, ChatGPT wasn't developed to do student's homework.)

To my surprise, she offered an unexpected solution. She invited me to her office after class, where she said she would personally assist me with the essay writing process once all classes were done.

My high school used to end all classes by 4 PM. Both students and teachers would go home around that time. However, Mrs. Backfield stayed at the school until 11 PM to help me with my essay. Not just me, she helped other international students too. I was grateful for her dedication, so I asked her for a recommendation letter as well. I had grown to like Mrs. Backfield.

Eventually, I had prepared everything, from my SAT and school grades to the recommendation letters. However, the most challenging part was writing the personal essay. The personal essay required reflecting on personal experiences and crafting one's unique narrative. Selecting a meaningful topic and uncovering insights from it were crucial. So, the personal essay demanded more time for thinking than actual writing.

But I was so focused on improving my SAT scores that I hadn't even thought about the personal essay. I assumed it would be a simple task since it was just one page long. I thought I could write it quickly during a lunch break at school.

However, I soon realized the essay's significance. Some colleges placed more importance on the personal essay than on school grades or SAT scores. It was the best way to gauge an applicant's creativity and uniqueness.

At that time, I hadn't done anything particularly remarkable. My daily routine consisted of going to school, playing soccer, and sleeping. I rarely ventured outside of my school life. Writing the personal essay felt like trying to cook a meal only with water. What could I make except for boiling water? How could I write an impressive essay when I hadn't done anything extraordinary?

In reality, the personal essay wasn't about being perfect in grammar or having exceptional comprehension skills like the SAT. It was more about having creative thoughts and ideas. If someone had a unique perspective, he could score well on it.

"I can do something like this." That's all I needed to show to colleges. Adding unique experiences to creative ideas could make my personal essay even better. Universities highly valued not only creative thinking but also extraordinary experiences.

However, I hadn't had any unique experiences in my life, especially during my high school years. So, I decided to get involved in new activities at school.

That's when I came across an advertisement promoted by the school – the "Make-A-Wish" organization.

Our school was well-known for its soccer team, but the band was also extremely popular. It included not only instrumentalists but also singers. The singers, in particular, had voices that were so pure and captivating that it was impossible not to love them. Even the birds in Cinderella animation had to be jealous of their voices.

Our band was quite large. It attracted a diverse group of individuals. Additionally, our school offered band classes, where students could receive proper music education. I learned music in South Korea, but it was mostly music theories. I didn't have much time to learn how to play instruments.

I had never really tried playing an instrument properly before coming to the United States. I had played cheap instruments I found in stationery stores a few times, but even those I couldn't play properly. People had to close their ears whenever I played them.

In the band class, I learned how to play instruments properly. Unlike music class in my middle school, the band only taught how to play instruments. As a result, the band class was a completely new and shocking experience for me. Music had always been something I only listened to; I had never been involved in creating or performing it myself.

Playing an instrument allowed me to feel the charm of music firsthand. It was surprisingly demanding. I had to use my fingers and lips extensively. I played the saxophone, which required a lot of breath control and finger movements according to the sheet music. It was not a lightweight instrument. My arms ached after practicing. However, as I became able to play songs, I fell in love with the saxophone. I had a few favorite songs that I enjoyed playing, like The Beatles' "Hey Jude" and a Korean artist called Yurisangja's "Magic Castle." It was fortunate that I had practiced these songs enough to play them myself.

At first, I didn't think I would be able to play the saxophone properly. The melodies of my favorite songs were so beautiful that it seemed impossible for me to recreate them. Somehow, I felt like I wouldn't be able to play them at all. However, as I began playing the simplest melodies, I realized how incredible the world of music was. With a bit of effort, I, too, could become a performer like everyone else. Anyone could step into uncharted territory with a little effort. It was almost like magic. If wizards needed wands, musicians needed instruments. In some ways, music was like magic, as it had the power to change people's feelings just by playing it.

In our school's band, many activities were taking place. The students in the band weren't just striving to become skilled musicians; they also wanted to showcase their music to others.

Fortunately, the band provided them with a platform to express their passion and creativity. One of the spaces that provided such opportunities was the "Make A Wish" Foundation. The "Make A Wish" Foundation helped people with wishes they couldn't fulfill on their own. They could request assistance from the foundation for their wishes. However, there were countless wishes in the world, so the foundation often sought collaborators to help grant these wishes.

I hadn't heard of the "Make A Wish" Foundation before, so I didn't know what it was about. With a name like "Make A Wish," I assumed it had something to do with granting wishes. I even thought about asking if they could make $10 billions appear in my bank account. However, the foundation wasn't about fulfilling whimsical wishes like mine. They weren't genies of the lamp.

The "Make A Wish" Foundation was an organization that helped children suffering from incurable diseases. For example, they would invite celebrities to entertain friends who had terminal illnesses or request performances from groups like our school's band.

Honestly, collaborating with such a noble foundation felt like a unique experience. Moreover, granting someone's wish was a meaningful endeavor to me. If I could make someone's wish come true through my efforts, I believed it would make me happy too. So, I became interested in participating in projects with the "Make A Wish" Foundation.

The project with the "Make A Wish" Foundation took place every summer vacation. Our school's band would travel to distant areas during summer vacation to perform for people who wanted to hear our music and then return. This summer, the project's goal was to perform for a child in Europe who had leukemia.

Around the time of summer vacation, auditions for the band started. Those who were selected could participate in the project with the "Make A Wish" Foundation.

I wanted to be one of the students selected for the band. However, there was one problem: my musical skills. I had only recently started playing the saxophone. I hadn't taken band classes in 9th or 10th grade. I only started taking them in 11th grade. So, I couldn't play many songs.

But there was a solution. In the band, not everyone had to be a perfect musician. We also needed people who could play harmony, called Second Players. While First Players played the basic melody, Second Players added harmonies that made the music more captivating. Harmony was like a conversation. Good conversation requires fluent speakers, but it became complete when it had nice listeners. Conversation became complete when the listeners gave a nice reaction. Thus, Second Players played significant role as well. They made spice to the rhytm made by First Players.

Fortunately, Second Players could be students with limited experience like me, so I was able to participate in the "Make A Wish" Foundation's project as a Second Player. The "Make A Wish" Foundation project took place during summer vacation because it couldn't be done during the school semester. This made me a bit disappointed because I could skip classes if the project was held during the semester.

Shortly after the last performance, the semester ended. I finally finished my junior year and was about to become a 12th grader, the senior who could clear the way in the high school. I heard a senior could do so in 'Kim Possible', an animation made by Disney. But in reality, there was no one clearing the path for me. Maybe the director of the animation went to a different high school from mine.

Once the semester ended, the dormitory supervisors all went home. The dormitories were not operational during the summer vacation, so there was no need for dormitory supervisors to stay at school.

Typically, there were no international students who stayed at school during the summer vacation. International students returned home during the summer vacation. If any of them had participated in the "Make A Wish" project, they could have stayed with me. However, I was the only international student from my school who participated in the "Make A Wish" project.

In college, they offered classes during summer vacation. Thus, the dormitories in college were operational. However, I was still a high school student. It wasn't possible for high school students to take summer classes. Therefore, the most challenging aspect of summer vacation for me was living alone in the dormitory until the project began. It felt quite lonely.

The "Make A Wish" project started about a week after our school's summer vacation began. During the summer break, there was no one else at the school. Fortunately, there was one dormitory supervisor who remained on campus to keep an eye on me. He was assigned to live with me to ensure my well-being during the summer vacation. However, even the dormitory supervisor rarely left his room to see me. He only brought me food during meal times. Still, I was grateful for his presence. Vacations for students were breaks for him as well. He had to work during his break to stay with me, but he didn't express any kind of dissatisfaction. I didn't want to disturb him further, so I mostly kept to myself. Consequently, until the "Make A Wish" project started, I got used to living alone.

I had to become accustomed to spending time by myself since there wasn't much to do alone. Even practicing my beloved soccer skills alone was not enjoyable. Therefore, I turned to the online world to find friends, especially in online games where it was easy to make friends. So, before the "Make A Wish" project began, I was busy defeating villains and helping game characters in the gaming world. If someone's wish was to defeat villains and protect the earth, I had already fulfilled that wish.

As time passed, my loneliness became more painful. It was around that time that the "Make A Wish" project began.

CHAPTER 7

● ● ● ● ● ● ●

The "Make A Wish" project wasn't exclusive to my school; students from other schools also participated in it. One of the reasons why the project couldn't start immediately after my school's summer vacation was because it involved students from other schools. Their summer vacations also had to begin for the project to proceed.

Since students from other schools were participating in the project, there was a need for joint rehearsals with my school's students. Students from other schools and my school needed to spend at least a few days together at our school to coordinate and get used to each other's performances. We had to become familiar with each other's music. After all, once we went to Europe, we wouldn't have the opportunity to practice together.

The students who participated in the project stayed in the

dormitories that were previously occupied by the international students for some time. Our school had plenty of dormitories for international students, so there was no shortage of rooms. The rooms were cleaned thoroughly before the international students left, so there were no issues there. The dormitory supervisors made sure the cleaning was done properly. Thanks to them, I did a lot of cleaning myself. I didn't know how to keep things tidy, so the dormitory supervisors often asked me to clean my room again. I needed things to be a bit messy for me to feel comfortable. Maybe my ancestor was a bacterium after all?

The friends who gathered at my school for the "Make A Wish" project were incredibly diverse. There were middle school students and friends who had come from Mexico. I lived in the same dormitory with the Mexican friends and got to know them well. They were really cheerful people. It was fortunate to share the same dormitory with such friendly individuals.

The students from other schools were quite skilled in playing music. Even though we hadn't known each other for long, we could play music together without any awkward notes. When talented musicians got together, they could create a masterpiece even in a short amount of time. Music was truly a powerful language.

After the students from other schools joined, we all spent five more days together before departing for Europe. There were around 50 students participating in the project. Many of them were from my school. However, the other students also played crucial roles in the project. They were greatly appreciated.

When we left the school, many parents gathered to see us off. There were no parents from the other schools, just the parents of my school's students. Nevertheless, there were so many of them that they filled the view outside the bus windows. Seeing the parents wishing us well reminded me of my own parents back in South Korea. I felt a strong sense of longing. I wanted to visit my country.

120

When we arrived at the airport, there were so many people that we couldn't all move together. With around 50 people, it was impossible for us all to move together anywhere. We took up too much space. However, our band teacher came up with a good idea. He suggested dividing people into smaller groups and having them proceed separately. This way, everyone could go through the check-in process without any issues. I also went through the check-in process smoothly while working with my Mexican friends in a smaller group.

However, I noticed something at the airport. My Mexican friends kept using English instead of their native language, Spanish, whenever I was around. It was then that I realized they were being considerate by not using Spanish in my presence. They were not so comfortable with using English. Thus, I intentionally distanced myself and pretended to have other things to do, leaving their group. I didn't want my friends to be uncomfortable because of me.

Once I was alone, I didn't have much to do. I had initially planned to wander around the airport until it was time to board the plane. But during that time alone, I made a new friend.

She was Kelly.

Kelly was quite a well-known figure at school. The reason for her popularity in school was her exemplary school life. She was an outstanding student.

She belonged to what I called the "Exemplary Student Club." In our school, there were a few exceptional students. I used to call them the Exemplary Student Club members. It was a nickname I gave them. They were like perfect students in every way.

The Exemplary Student Club members were nothing short of elite. They excelled both academically and in terms of their character. Thanks to that, they had many friends and were the ones representing the school.

I learned about the Exemplary Student Club members when I took AP classes at school. Our school had a program that allowed us to take university-level courses. These courses were called AP classes, and they were quite challenging for high school students.

The reason for taking such challenging courses was simple. There were rewards associated with them. AP classes provided a grade point boost. If I scored above a certain level, universities recognized the AP classes I took, which meant I didn't have to take the same courses in college. For example, if I scored well in AP history, I didn't have to take a history course in college.

Our school courses were broadly divided into three categories. The most straightforward courses were "Regular" classes, which were at the typical high school level. Most students often took these classes. One step up in difficulty was the "Honors" classes, which were slightly more challenging than standard high school classes. These classes were tough to get good grades in. Still, they added a 15% boost to GPA. The most challenging courses were the AP classes. These classes added a 30% boost to GPA.

The extra points for AP classes were so tempting that I tried signing up for AP History once. I had received good grades in History Honors, so I thought I could take on the challenge. However, my confidence took a massive hit. In AP History, I had to read a staggering 40 pages of the textbook every day just to keep up with the class. The textbook wasn't small by any means. Even carrying one in my bag was a shoulder-straining task. Each page of the textbook was massive. The content was extensive. Reading 40 pages of such a colossal book every day was no easy feat. Moreover, merely reading wasn't enough; I had to memorize all that content to write exams without any reference material. The process of studying for that class was excruciating. It felt like my head was about to explode. Hitting my head with that enormous textbook would hurt less.

But there were some students in that class who seemed to be

completely at ease. They were none other than the Exemplary Student Club members. In a class where I felt like my brain was being stolen, they appeared to be completely relaxed.

During AP History class, I never put my pen down. I did it to ensure I didn't miss writing what the teacher said. So, I diligently jotted down whatever the teacher mentioned. And when those topics came up in exams, I got them all wrong like a possessed person.

On the other hand, the Exemplary Student Club members didn't seem to need to write anything. They simply nodded when the teacher spoke. I was always so busy taking notes that I couldn't fathom how they managed to remember everything from the class. Watching those students nod along during the class without writing anything down was fascinating. Without taking notes, it seemed impossible to remember the class content. Yet, they always seemed to know it perfectly.

I thought studying like them was a wise approach, so I tried attending a class like they did once. I just listened and occasionally nodded along with the teacher. Then, during the exam, I had to write nothing and only nod my head. Ironically, during exams, the Exemplary Student Club members wrote furiously as if possessed. They clearly weren't the ones who wrote much during class. How could they remember all the class content? Were we taking the same class?

I put my soul into that class and, on the first exam, I failed. But I didn't give up; I kept trying. Then, on the second exam, I failed again. Still, I wasn't disheartened. Hope always finds a way. And on the third exam, I finally failed once more. That's when I decided to withdraw from the class. I knew that giving up wasn't good. Still, I had an excuse. I didn't give up AP History. Instead, AP History gave me up.

Actually, the reason I decided to withdraw was because of some of those Exemplary Student Club members. I overheard them saying something on the day I failed the exam.

"This exam was quite easy, don't you think?"

Hearing them say that made me think I might never be able to handle AP History. The class seemed tailored for students like those in the Exemplary Student Club.

Anyway, those Exemplary Student Club members were like they were from a different world. Somehow, they even hung out exclusively among themselves. Their conversations were slow and deliberate, making their surroundings feel like time was moving in slow motion. If there was a remote control, I would have fast-forwarded their conversations by 1.5 times.

I thought I would have no chance to become friends with those Exemplary Student Club members. We belonged in different world. Still, I had once been close to a member of the Exemplary Student Club. Unfortunately, it just didn't work out in the end.

Among the Exemplary Student Club members was a middle school student who wore a red t-shirt. This kid was incredibly cheerful and got along well with everyone. Being around her, it was harder not to smile than to smile.

She was someone who approached others first and was always kind to me since I first arrived. Initially, I was really grateful to the girl in the red t-shirt. I was quite lonely living abroad.

Her way of greeting people was also unique. She expressed her joy with her whole heart when she greeted someone. The girl in the red t-shirt was even more delighted to greet me. Her welcoming presence meant so much to me. Even my dog at home didn't seem as happy to see me even when I gave him treats.

She was an honest person. Perhaps she lived her life honestly, which allowed her to be so open about her feelings. If there were more people like her in this world, it would be a brighter place.

However, what caused me to distance myself from her was nothing other than my own insecurities. I couldn't accept her sincere feelings.

The girl in the red t-shirt had a heart as clear as water. Within that transparency, I couldn't find a trace of malice. Even the snow couldn't be as clear as her heart.

But the reason I couldn't accept such a beautiful heart was simple. When I looked at her, I couldn't help but think of how different I was from her. She was like still water, so pure that I could only see my own impurities reflected in her.

I wasn't someone who liked myself. I lacked self-confidence. As a result, I started to worry. I thought she might eventually see my true self. I was not a good person. I was a coward who usually betrayed my own friends. Somehow, I felt like she would see through all my pretense. I was afraid she would be disappointed. And if a good person like her started to dislike me, it would be too painful.

In short, I lacked courage. So, I started avoiding her. I didn't have the confidence to live as honestly as she did.

I also tried to change. She really was a great person. So, I didn't want to show that I was avoiding her. I wanted to show her the changed me. I wanted to have self-love, be someone who could smile and say hello to her. And I wanted to ask her if I could become her friend someday.

But before I could do that, she left. She sensed that I was uncomfortable around her. She was really good at reading people's feelings. She realized that I was avoiding her, and she ended up not liking me anymore. What was I so afraid of?

That girl with the red T-shirt was outgoing even among the Exemplary Student Club members. Everyone in the club liked her, and she played a role in bridging the gap between me and the Exemplary Student Club members. However, as my relationship with her became strained, I distanced myself from the club members as well. So, I thought I no longer had a connection with the Exemplary Student Club members.

But by chance, I became quite close again with one of them, Kelly, at the airport. We had a few conversations, which was rare for me with a club member. It was just small talk, but regardless of the content, I was pleased to have a relationship where I could talk to someone again.

As the time came to board the plane, Kelly returned to the other Exemplary Student Club members. They were quite involved in the 'Make A Wish' project. When Kelly went back to the Exemplary Student Club members, I thought our connection would end. We weren't that close, after all. However, before parting ways, she said something.

"See you again."

I thought I wouldn't have any more relationships with the Exemplary Student Club members. But the future was always something I could never know.

"Make A Wish" project participants boarded a large bus after getting off the plane. It was even larger than the buses we used to get from school to the airport. It was a massive two-story bus.

The first floor was reserved for students who were sociable and had strong leadership qualities. They were mostly seniors. They shared the first floor with teachers. The rest of the students took seats on the second floor. Since the second floor had more seats, many students sat there.

As I mentioned before, the teachers divided the students into various groups even at the airport. They appointed a leader for each group. The leaders were usually the ones seated on the first floor.

The leader of the group I was in was quite humorous. When we arrived in Europe, he went to buy bright red underwear. He claimed that he had to buy a gift for his girlfriend. However, I thought he was lying. He was the only one who would appreciate his girlfriend wearing it. He was buying a gift for himself. Thus, I started to like him.

The band didn't visit famous tourist destinations in Europe. Instead, we explored enjoyable places that most people didn't know about. It all started with a small elementary school in the UK. When the I first arrived at the elementary school, all I could see around me were trees. It was literally a school built by cutting down trees on a mountainside. The village where the school was located was situated on the mid-level of the mountain. Therefore, the land wasn't very spacious, as it wasn't a city area. Because of this, the students in the school didn't have many opportunities to interact with people from other regions. For growing children, interacting with the outside world was essential as they learned about the world's various aspects.

Our school took the initiative to help those children. Our band members decided to go to that school and perform for the kids. If the kids couldn't come to our school or city for some reason, we would go to them.

We gathered on the elementary school's playground to start our performance. Since it was not a very large school, there were more band members than students. However, that fact didn't matter. The smiles on the kids' faces were so beautiful. Watching their pure smiles made us feel like we were all back in elementary school ourselves.

Our band teacher was very smart. Suddenly, he started calling a few band members, including me. Then he told us that we didn't need to perform. He thought it would be better to perform with a smaller group since the space was small, and there were many people. He said that we would have a chance to play in the next destination.

The role of those of us called by the band teacher was to play with the kids. The teacher had a brilliant idea. Kids enjoyed playing with people the most. Especially when adults liked them, the kids became even happier.

We played only joyful songs. Many band members started mingling with the kids. We made sure that we hung around with all the kids. After all, it's not a party if someone is left alone. The essence of a festival is that everyone is happy.

Playing with those who were alone quickly lifted their spirits. They became happy and started dancing together.

I had no idea how to dance at all. I knew it would be a problem when I eventually went on a formal date with a woman. I didn't know how to dance or sing at all. However, even someone like me had no problem dancing with the kids. The elementary school students were incredible dancers. I simply followed the dance moves the kids were doing. If I moved my feet to match their steps, that was dancing.

'Shall we dance?'

It felt like the footprints created by the children and our band members were speaking.

We also had meals together with the children. The school treated us to a meal as a token of appreciation. It was a meal made from ingredients found in the mountains. I could taste the flavors of nature. Especially the salad topped with cheese was something that made me want to visit that place again.

We hadn't been at the school for very long, but it felt like we had already become close to the children. So, the moment of parting was quite sad.

As the time to leave approached, some people had already started packing. We had a lot of diligent friends in our band who didn't hesitate to do hard work. They were the unsung heroes of our band. I thought it was great to help them. So, we started cleaning up together.

While we were cleaning up, a child approached and asked for

an autograph on her shirt. I was taken aback at that moment. I didn't have a particularly cool autograph. I had never thought there would be a need for an autograph in my life. I hadn't practiced it.

However, since I was asked, I wanted to give her an autograph. I thought for a moment and wrote down the autograph that came to my mind.

'

The autograph I wrote was, "To my dearest friend," which wasn't anything particularly special. I wrote it in Korean because it seemed like the child had never seen the language before. Upon receiving the autograph, the child proudly showed it to the other kids. Although it wasn't a remarkable autograph, somehow it had become impressive. I was grateful that the child liked my autograph. It wasn't me who made the autograph cool; it was the child's happiness.

After the performance at the elementary school in the mountains, our band headed to the next destination. We didn't stay in the UK for long. The entire trip for the 'Make a Wish' project was only two weeks. We had to tour all of Europe, so time was limited. Europe has a lot of countries. We had a lot of ground to cover. From that day on, our band embarked on an intense journey.

We sometimes had to eat and sleep on the bus to cover long distances. Sleeping on the bus was a real challenge, at least for me. There were times when we had to fall asleep on the bus at night without having the chance to shower. It was such a pain. I hated sleeping without a shower.

However, traveling around the countries wasn't just a tough experience. Especially, crossing from the UK to other countries was exciting. We had to load the entire bus onto a ferry to cross to another country. When we first arrived at the port, we had to get off the bus. It was the band teacher's instruction. I was packing my belongings, thinking that it was time to say a sad goodbye to the bus. However, the band teacher smiled and said there was no need for that. He said that we were going to board the exact same bus again.

The band teacher often made jokes. After falling for a few of them, I never trusted him. Once, he recommended that I try playing a strange instrument. The name of the instrument was so strange that it was hard to remember. It didn't take long for me to give up playing the instrument. It was even larger than I was. When I tried blowing into it, not even a whistling sound came out. The band teacher was laughing at me as I struggled to play it. After that, I didn't trust the band teacher's words much.

So, when the band teacher said I could leave my luggage on the bus and board the ferry, I didn't believe him. I told the teacher with a smile that I would leave the luggage on the bus and board the ferry. I had to pretend to trust the teacher because he often joked. So, in reality, I packed all my luggage. I thought the band teacher must be deceiving me. I had never seen a bus being loaded onto a ferry like this in my life. It was hard to imagine how they could load such a heavy bus onto a ferry.

But when I actually boarded the ferry, I was the only one who had packed my luggage. I did see a few others packing their luggage, but there were too few of them. I couldn't understand why people weren't packing their luggage. And as soon as we arrived in Germany, I found out why. Upon arriving in Germany, we boarded the exact same bus we had in the UK.

When we boarded the bus in Germany, I thought it just looked similar to the one we had in the UK. But it turned out to be the same bus we had ridden from the UK. Just as the band teacher had said, our bus had crossed to another country on a ferry. I realized I needed to develop the skill to distinguish between the teacher's jokes and truths. I kept believing the band teacher's jokes were truths, and when he told the truth, I thought it was a joke.

After arriving in Germany, we visited many countries, including France, Belgium, Austria, and more. There was hardly any European country left unvisited by us. Of course, we could only stay in most of these countries for a day or two, but it was quite an experience.

Traveling to so many countries in Europe was exhausting. Our energy was often drained, especially when spending several hours on the bus each day. However, being with friends made a big difference. Sitting on the bus for long hours allowed us to become close to those sitting nearby. So, chatting and having fun with them during the journey often gave us a boost of energy, even during challenging times.

On the buses we traveled in Europe, people rarely changed seats. Most passengers left their luggage in their seats and disembarked. When they returned, they would go back to their assigned seats. As a result, I kept running into the same friends when getting back on the bus. This made it easy for everyone to become friends with those who sat next to them. Continuous meetings made it easy for people to become friends.

The front seats on the upper floor of the bus were reserved for the oldest band members. They had more life experience, even though they were still students. They were experienced in managing situations to prevent problems. When people on the bus became too noisy, they quietly handled the situation. They acted as leaders in a way.

The front seat on the lower floor was occupied by the bus driver. In reality, the bus driver often had to drive alone even when all the band members were asleep. The people sitting at the front of the upper floor were in close proximity to the bus driver. Therefore, they needed to be calm and considerate, refraining from making too much noise to avoid disturbing the driver. Sitting in the front seat on the upper floor required a sense of responsibility and maturity.

Of course, sitting in the front seat on the upper floor could be seen as a burdensome duty. They had to manage the students on the upper floor if they were too loud. Nevertheless, those who sat in the front seats had their own privileges. They could enjoy the breathtaking views of Europe through the large front window, unobstructed by curtains. Being able to take in Europe's beautiful landscapes at a glance was a significant privilege.

As for my seat, I was sitting towards the back of the bus, but not all the way in the last row.

At the very back of the bus, there was a restroom. It was probably because it was a long-distance bus that it had a restroom on board. Although it was somewhat unique, there was indeed a restroom on the bus. However, hardly anyone used the restroom. It wasn't built for the large number of passengers on the bus. It was meant to be used only in unavoidable situations. So, I had never seen anyone on the trip using the bus's restroom. Thanks to that, sitting near the restroom wasn't a big problem. Since hardly anyone used it, there was no smell or dirtiness to worry about.

However, there were people sitting near me, in a similar location. They were the Exemplary Student Club members. Among them, Kelly was there. She was a friend I had talked to at the airport when we were traveling to Europe together.

I didn't have many opportunities to socialize with the Exemplary Student Club members at school. Since I kept my distance from the girl with the red shirt, the Exemplary Student Club member, I didn't have a chance to be friends with them.

Among the Exemplary Student Club members I knew at school, there were Kelly, the girl with the red shirt, and the 'Male-Female Couple.' The 'Male-Female Couple' was a nickname I made for the couple who were always together. They were the Exemplary Student Club members who were very comfortable in their AP History class, which I failed and withdrew from. Both of them were taking the same AP History class that I was. They were the ones who had said, 'This test was quite easy,' after a test that I had failed.

They were inseparable at school. So, the Male-Female Couple was often seen together on the streets as well. Although I had seen many couples, the Male-Female Couple seemed to have a deeper affection for each other. They would look at each other and smile without saying anything. I couldn't understand the reason behind their laughter every time they looked at each other. Perhaps they had made a pact that one of them would shoot the other if they didn't smile?

In the back seats of the bus, I encountered another Exemplary Student Club member aside from the Male-Female Couple and Kelly. It was the Saxophone First Player. I was one of the Saxophone Second Players in the band, responsible for adding harmony. In contrast, he was the First Player, known for truly understanding the nuances of playing the saxophone. He was famous for excelling not only in music but also in academics. Thus, I appointed him as a member of Exemplary Student Club. I made up the club, so I could appoint anyone I wanted. Of course, none of the Exemplary Student Club members knew that I had appointed them.

In the very back of the bus, there were four consecutive seats. The rest of the seats were divided into pairs with an aisle in the middle. Thanks to this arrangement, the Exemplary Student Club members could all sit together in the very back seats.

During the trip, I met a friend who enjoyed playing the same game I did. Since I only played games on the bus during the journey, I wasn't particularly interested in others. One day, I encountered a friend who had the same gaming device as me. So, we spent the entire day playing games together on the bus.

The game we played was called 'Pokemon,' a game where I threw strange baseball-like objects to catch monsters I encountered on the street. If I were lucky, the monsters would be caught inside the baseball. That's when they became my friends. In simple terms, 'Pokemon' was a game about abducting wild animals.

They probably had families too, but the fun of the game was kidnapping them and traveling together. Still, it was quite amazing that they could become my friends once they were inside the baseball. Of course, the most astonishing thing was that creatures much larger than me could fit inside a baseball. Newton, the physics master, would have been surprised if he had a chance to play it.

In Europe, it felt like we were saving the world every day just by playing Pokemon. The game had villains who wanted to conquer the world. Surprisingly, the Pokemon villains were quite dedicated. They always wanted to settle things with monsters, never engaging in direct combat themselves. So, the most challenging weapon they developed was a baseball that could catch any monster in one go. I might have created a nuclear bomb if I were in their shoes. Maybe those villains were surprisingly naive.

While I spent my time defeating villains, there were also changes in the Exemplary Student Club members. At first, I didn't notice, but at some point, one of the members changed. Specifically, a friend named Jessie took the seat where the Saxophone First Player used to sit.

CHAPTER 8

* * * * * * * *

Usually, students didn't change their seats on the bus once they had settled during the trip. However, there had to be an exception when we arrived in Germany.

In Germany, we traveled with a friend who had leukemia on the bus. Helping him was the main purpose of the trip. We needed to arrange the best possible space on the bus for our friend with leukemia, so the Saxophone First Player gave up his seat.

The back seats of the bus were a space where everyone could see each other's faces. As soon as people turned around, they could see our friend with leukemia.

We met our friend in a square. We seated our friend with leukemia in the best spot to watch the performance and started playing music. Many spectators gathered, but the best seat was reserved for our friend with leukemia.

After the performance, we took our friend with leukemia back on the bus. We spent half a day traveling together. Apart from our band members and staff, our friend with leukemia was the only person on our bus.

That friend was always smiling and looked at everything with wonder. Sometimes, when looking out of the bus window, he had curious and fascinated eyes, like a child discovering things for the first time. It seemed as though he was seeing things in the world as if they were brand new. I wondered what he was seeing that made him so fascinated. So, I tried looking out the window as well. However, outside, there were just the usual buildings and roads that I saw every day. But for that friend, even such ordinary scenery seemed incredibly fascinating. He wore a very happy expression while gazing at it. It appeared that he found looking at the ordinary landscapes from the bus genuinely enjoyable. Seeing his bright demeanor, it felt like everyone on the bus was overflowing with positive energy.

At first, I didn't even know that this friend had leukemia. When we were traveling together, everyone was sharing laughter that anyone could join in on. Among the friends, those with small instruments would introduce their instruments on the bus and play songs for us. Listening to their performances on the bus was truly delightful. The friend we invited onto our bus responded with a smile when he heard those songs.

A smile was the energy of life. When someone smile, it gives him strength. Only those with strength can smile. So, I thought that this friend was very healthy. I thought he had almost recovered from his illness. I believed that an illness wouldn't be able to harm the smile.

We explored the city together. After some time, we reached the same spot where we first met this friend. We all said our goodbyes and wished him well. I also hoped for a bright future for this friend.

Even as we parted ways, this friend continued to smile and wave. I wondered how happy he must be to be able to smile every moment. If possible, I wanted to capture his smile in a little box and take it home with me. If that wasn't possible, I wished I could ask him to visit our school at least once.

However, I couldn't make such a request. A few days later, this friend passed away.

Our friend with leukemia passed away. That's what our band teacher told us a few days after leaving Germany. We were in the middle of traveling from France to Austria after just finishing a show.

It was a moment like any other, spending time on the bus with friends nearby. But suddenly, our band teacher came up to the second floor of the bus and said those words.

I initially misunderstood what our band teacher meant. I wasn't familiar with the concept of death. It was something I had only read about in books. I couldn't grasp that it actually existed. When we heard about our friend with leukemia, I was in the midst of having fun with my friends. So, I wasn't fully focused on what our band teacher was saying.

I thought my limited English skills had caused a misunderstanding. Our band teacher had a somber expression, which was unusual. After telling us that our friend with leukemia had passed away, he went back downstairs, looking unusually subdued for someone usually full of energy.

I couldn't accept the reality for a moment. It was too sudden. I believed that someone leaving this world wouldn't happen to someone related to me. I thought, 'Surely it can't be true.' So, I looked around for a moment, expecting that one of my friends, who always wore a cheerful expression, would be nearby. I intended to ask that friend what our band teacher had meant. I thought he would say, 'Nothing happened.'

But for some reason, all the people around me had gloomy expressions. The usual joy and enthusiasm of the friends who played their instruments had disappeared. It was only then that I realized I had understood our band teacher's words correctly.

I used to think the world was beautiful. I believed everyone could overcome any pain. But it seemed that the world was crueler than I had thought.

Our friend who had leukemia was in great pain throughout the time we spent together. He was preparing for his final farewell to the world. He wanted to know what the world was like outside of the hospital, just before leaving it for the last time.

If only I had known, I would have shared more stories that would have piqued his curiosity. I couldn't bring myself to say those things at the time.

When our band teacher informed us about our friend with leukemia, many students accepted the news quietly. Especially the Exemplary Student Club members seemed to have some expectations, as they had spent time with the sick friend from the beginning. Somehow, it seemed like our band teacher indirectly informed them about the condition of our friend with leukemia from the start. Perhaps our band teacher had told them in a way that indicated he wouldn't last long due to leukemia. I guessed that he may have asked them to be considerate of our friend who had leukemia as much as possible.

A vacant seat appeared at the very back of the bus. It was the seat our friend with leukemia used to sit in. Originally, it was a seat for the Saxophone First Player. However, he had willingly given up his seat for our friend with leukemia. It was the best seat on the bus where everyone could be seen.

At some point, the Saxophone First Player moved to the front seats of the bus. However, even after our friend with leukemia passed away, the Saxophone First Player didn't return to his original seat. He continued to stay in the front seat as usual, leaving a vacant seat at the back of our bus.

Then, after a few days had passed, I was about to get on the bus after finishing another performance, just as always. I was heading to my seat when I noticed something different from usual. The seat at the back of the bus, which had been empty, was now occupied. A girl named Jessie was sitting there.

Jessie was a friend I hadn't seen before joining the Exemplary Student Club. We had only seen each other's faces when I was in the band. We had never really talked.

At first, I thought Jessie had just come to sit in the back seat for a day or so. I assumed she would return to her seat shortly. However, as time passed, she continued to stay in that seat. Eventually, it became familiar to see her in that seat. She had become the owner of that seat.

However, I didn't have a chance to have a conversation with Jessie. I usually talked to my friend in the seat next to mine. Jessie, too, seemed to talk mainly with her friends, like Kelly and the Male-Female couple who sat next to her, who were also Exemplary Student Club members.

Then, I had an opportunity to get to know Jessie better. It happened when we all went to an amusement park together with the Exemplary Student Club members.

During our travels in Europe, there was a time when our band teacher once gave us a chance to take a break and enjoy ourselves at an amusement park. We hadn't really had the opportunity to explore Europe, a beautiful continent, properly. There was no travel but only performance in the 'Make A Wish' project. Beside the Vikings, who chose to invade rather than to travel, we had to be the only ones who didn't travel in Europe. So, our band teacher arranged a special time for us to have fun as a reward for our hard work.

The amusement park wasn't that big, but it was enough for us to have a great time. Even though it was getting close to evening, there weren't many people in the amusement park. As a result, we had the perfect time to enjoy ourselves.

However, my friend who usually hung out with me on the bus had gone with some other people to have fun. He was the friend I always played games with. I thought of following him, but the group he joined was too crowded. Therefore, I decided to see if there was another group I could join. I didn't like being in large crowds at amusement parks.

Thus, I got off the bus and looked around. That's when I saw the Exemplary Student Club members getting off the bus. It was a group of four, including the Male-Female couple, Kelly, and Jessie. I thought they were all going into the amusement park together. However, the Male-Female couple split up and went into the amusement park separately. It seemed they had other plans.

It appeared that they were the last ones to get off the bus. So, I tried to see if there was a group among those who had already entered the amusement park that I could join. I wanted to join the Exemplary Student Club members, but we weren't close to each other.

Then, Kelly, who noticed that I was alone, came over. She thought I didn't have anyone to go with.

"Hoon, do you want to join us?"

I stared at her for a moment and then nodded. And that's how my trip to the amusement park with Kelly, and Jessie began.

I had never really befriended popular people before. I usually made friends with quiet and shy individuals. So, I had this fantasy about popular people; they seemed like they would be something special. But talking with Kelly and Jessie, I couldn't find anything particularly unique about them. In fact, they were just regular people who got angry at annoying things and laughed at funny ones, just like everyone else. Maybe blending in with ordinary things and people was the recipe for getting along well with others?

I spent time at the amusement park with them. I was really happy that I had made good friends. We went on various rides, some of which were so thrilling that they made my stomach churn. Fortunately, I didn't end up vomiting. It was lucky that I hadn't eaten much for lunch that day.

While we were having a blast at the amusement park, I suddenly felt like having ice cream. It was scorching hot that day, so I thought about getting some ice cream from a nearby shop. I also planned to buy some for my two friends, Kelly and Jessie, as I thought they might appreciate something to cool them down.

We were standing in line to ride bumper cars, a fun attraction where cars bump into each other. I wondered who came up with the idea of creating a ride where cars crash into each other. I had always thought that cars shouldn't collide with each other. Could it be that the person who came up with bumper cars was an insurance fraudster? I couldn't think of anyone else besides an insurance fraudster who would want cars to crash into each other.

I told Kelly and Jessie that I would go get something to eat for us. They told me to take my time. Luckily, I found a decent-looking ice cream shop nearby. I ordered three ice creams. Since I didn't know what flavors Kelly and Jessie liked, I decided to go with chocolate ice cream. Chocolate was universally loved.

I was on my way back with the ice creams when I started to see the line for the bumper cars in the distance. I began looking for Kelly and Jessie. The line had moved a bit while I was buying the ice creams, so Kelly and Jessie were in a different position now.

Finally, I spotted Kelly and Jessie. I waved at them. However, their demeanor seemed a bit strange. Kelly had her arm around Jessie's neck, and they were passionately kissing.

I turned away momentarily. I didn't know why, but it didn't feel right to see them in that moment. I felt like I had stumbled upon Kelly and Jessie's private moment. I wasn't sure if it was appropriate for me to witness it.

After a brief moment of contemplation, I decided to look back at them. Turning away felt like I was avoiding them. There was no reason to make a simple kiss seem strange. So, I turned back and saw that they were now separated, having a regular conversation, just like friends would. It was a completely ordinary interaction.

I joined them. They welcomed me just like they always did. However, I couldn't help but feel a bit uneasy compared to our usual interactions. The image of them kissing was still fresh in my mind. Women loving each other had always seemed forbidden to me. I had always avoided what society frowned upon. I didn't want to engage in anything that wasn't accepted, as it often led to hatred and rejection.

But after witnessing Kelly and Jessie's kiss, I found myself in conflict. I didn't know if I should accept them as friends or not. I had not been taught that same-sex love was allowed. Society generally didn't approve of it.

I wanted to be someone that others liked. Life was too difficult if people hated me. Going against what others said made the world a scary place. So, I aimed to be a good listener and agreed with everyone's opinions to avoid becoming the object of hatred. It was my way of surviving.

However, I couldn't bring myself to automatically agree with society's view on same-sex love, especially when it involved my friends. So, I decided to avoid the conflict once again. I pretended that I hadn't seen anything. I wanted to protect my friendship and avoid going against society's norms. It was a cowardly act, but I wanted to ensure my own well-being.

Not long after, our adventure at the amusement park came to an end. Everyone was returning to the bus. People were starting to take their seats. My friend who sat next to me also returned. I took my seat as well. Then, I turned to Kelly and Jessie and told them that I had a good time. They were sitting near me, so I could easily talk to them.

As soon as I greeted them, I immediately lay down in my seat. To be honest, I couldn't shake off the shock I had felt earlier. The image of Kelly and Jessie kissing was still vivid in my mind.

In fact, it wasn't just a shock. I didn't know how to act or face them. I was afraid of being called gay or lesbian if I supported Kelly and Jessie's relationship. So, I decided to pretend to be asleep, hoping that time would help me process everything. I just wanted to shut everything out and forget what I had witnessed earlier. I wished I could just fall asleep quickly. If there had been an anesthetic, I would have taken it just to escape this situation.

However, I soon heard voices from the back of the bus. It was the Exemplary Student Club members. At first, I didn't pay much attention to them; I didn't like eavesdropping on other people's conversations.

But that day, something about the voices of the Exemplary Student Club members sounded different. Specifically, the voice of the Male-Female couple sounded cautious.

They said, "Does Hoon know about you?"

Then, I heard Kelly's voice, which sounded surprisingly clear. She replied, "He probably knows now."

I didn't really hear what they were talking about. Still, I somehow knew that she talked about me knowing her relationship with Jessie.

I didn't know how to react to those words. I continued to lie there with my eyes closed, hoping desperately for sleep to come. Still, I couldn't fall asleep.

"Could it be that she brought it up on purpose for me to hear?"

While lying in my seat, this thought crossed my mind. However, I couldn't know the answer for sure. On one hand, I worried that Kelly might be testing me. Perhaps she wanted to see my true feelings. But in any case, I couldn't just dwell on it. The truth was, Kelly didn't seem likely to reveal it to me even if I asked.

My only concern was how to remain a good friend to her. I could ignore Kelly and Jessie's relationship if I wanted to. They weren't going to break our friendship just because I pretended like I didn't know about it. Still, could a friend pretend not to know their friend's true self?

I didn't know how to approach them. I couldn't just say, "I don't care who you're dating," because that might prompt them to ask, "Why do you even care in the first place?"

The simplest way for me was to ignore the complicated issue. Honestly, I had only become close to Kelly and Jessie recently; our friendship was relatively new. If the issue involving them became too troublesome, I could have simply chosen not to be friends with them anymore. But I didn't want that.

I was especially concerned about Kelly. She would create space for me whenever she noticed me alone. She was a smart person. She probably knew I wasn't the most socially adept individual. Yet, she pretended not to notice and embraced me with open arms. I was grateful for her kindness, and I wanted to be there for her when she needed support.

However, after the incident at the amusement park, I was unsure about how to face Kelly. I just wanted to greet her as if nothing had happened. But somehow, I felt like I needed to let her know what I thought about the situation, even though I couldn't find the right way to do it. I pondered over it, but no clear answer came to mind.

Strangely, it seemed like I didn't need to worry about it. The next day when I met Kelly, she greeted me warmly. We had spent the previous day at the amusement park and then stayed at a hotel overnight. In the morning, we all had breakfast at the hotel's buffet restaurant.

I encountered Kelly there, and I couldn't act naturally. I could feel tension rising inside my body. Even a greeting looked so artificial. I was worried if she noticed my strangeness. Still, I didn't have to make a natural conversation. When she saw me, she greeted me enthusiastically.

"Hi, Hoon!"

She was the same Kelly I had always known. But somehow, I felt like I couldn't be my usual self.

Our band arrived in a small castle town after having breakfast. It wasn't a performance venue; we just stopped by for some sightseeing. Our band teacher wanted to show the students a few more tourist spots.

He couldn't provide detailed explanations. Since I didn't care about history of any kind, I didn't need an explanation about 'how the castle town was built' or 'Who the Amazing made it.' All I wanted to do was to walk around and hope to find something distinct. Fortunately, that's all the band teacher wanted as well. After we looked around for a bit, he asked us to return to the bus.

To be honest, I wasn't particularly interested in the castle. My mind was filled with the image of Kelly and Jessie kissing that I had seen at the amusement park. No matter what I looked at, the scene of Kelly and Jessie locking lips was the only thing in my mind.

Fortunately, the castle sightseeing didn't give me much time to dwell on my thoughts. The castle was huge. There were an overwhelming number of stairs. So, while exploring the castle,

I didn't have time to think too much. By the time we left the castle, I was drenched in sweat. It was summer, and the castle didn't have proper ventilation. I felt like I was in a sauna. I could understand why the air conditioner was one of the most popular inventions in the world.

One fortunate thing was that there was an exit in the castle. The seemingly endless castle tour did come to an end.

After visiting the castle, our band had to move on to our next destination. So, we all headed to the bus.

At that moment, I just wanted to get on the bus quickly. I couldn't stand on my feet any longer. So, I tried to make my way back to the bus. However, I saw Kelly and Jessie in the distance. They were heading towards the bus before me.

I felt genuinely happy to see them. They were my friends. I decided to approach them and say hello. But at that moment, the image of Kelly and Jessie I had seen yesterday came back to me. I remembered how I had tried to act like I didn't see anything.

I wondered if I should greet them. To be honest, Kelly would have been easygoing if I greeted her. She would have remained just a comfortable friend if I wanted that. Perhaps she wouldn't have minded if I acted like I didn't see the scene at the amusement park. She was not the type to force something onto others; she allowed people to live as they wished.

But I couldn't just ignore what I knew. I had a feeling that Kelly, for some reason, couldn't talk openly about her relationship with Jessie. Maybe for her, that relationship was something she couldn't be straightforward about.

Thinking along those lines, it suddenly seemed like Kelly couldn't show me her vulnerable side. Most couples usually showed off their love excessively, but Kelly didn't seem to do that.

So, I suddenly rushed up to Kelly suddenly and grabbed her by the arm.

Kelly seemed surprised at first, but she quickly composed herself and greeted me with her usual bright smile.

"Hello, Hoon?"

Just like always, she greeted me with a cheerful demeanor.

"I'm not sure what I should say to you."

I began speaking abruptly without explaining the situation, pouring out the words from my mind.

"How you'll take what I say, I'm not quite sure," I said in a very serious tone, which seemed to slightly confuse Kelly. However, I didn't waver in my intent. I continued with what I wanted to say. Kelly's expression also changed somewhat. She was usually a cheerful friend, but now she looked at me with a serious expression.

Then I told her, "But can I still be your friend?"

I said it in a tone that seemed unsure of how to proceed further. In fact, I didn't mention anything about what I had seen with Kelly and Jessie the previous day. It was simply a question of whether it would be okay for us to be friends.

This kind of foolish proposal is unheard of. Who in the world would ask if it's okay to become friends? Even young children who have just started kindergarten wouldn't try to make friends like this. I clearly had issues with my social skills.

However, I really wanted to ask Kelly if it would be okay to be her friend. If I didn't say it, I felt like I was abandoning Kelly for some reason. I couldn't quite put my finger on why, but I felt like I was betraying my friend, Kelly, if I didn't ask her if I could be her friend. That's why I spoke to Kelly. I wanted to tell her that I wanted to be on my friend's side. I wasn't sure if I made the appropriate approach. Still, I believed that I had to convey her what I thought.

I thought I would come across as quite foolish. After all, I suddenly came to her asking if I could be her friend. It wasn't a usual way to make friends. I was worried that Kelly might dislike me for it. Not many people want to be friends with someone who can't even speak properly. Moreover, she could dislike someone who cared about her relationship with Jessie.

But I still wanted to talk about it. I wanted to share in my friend's worries. And for that, if our friendship had to end, then it couldn't be helped. It was regrettable, but I was willing to accept it. I believed that true friends cared more about their friends than about their relationship.

But before I could even have time to worry, Kelly started to laugh. I didn't know what it meant.

Then she said, "Of course!"

And we became friends.

After my time in Europe came to an end, I entered my fourth year of high school. Now, it was the time when I had to prepare for college admissions in earnest.

I wrote an admission essay, incorporating my experiences in Europe. The main focus of the essay was a leukemia patient's story. I was deeply moved by that child. Even in the toughest moments, he never seemed to lose hope. So, that friend kept coming to my mind.

And for some reason, I also wrote about Kelly. I didn't know that she could hold a special meaning for me. At least not during the moments when we first started talking.

However, I couldn't forget the moment when I asked Kelly if it would be okay to be her friend. It took a lot of courage to make that request, but surprisingly, the outcome wasn't bad. So, I included that fact in my essay. I wanted to show the university what kind of life I was living.

College acceptance announcements usually came before the end of the fourth year of the high school. After the acceptance notices were out, students didn't need to worry much about their academic performance. There was no need to strive for better grades in high school to submit to colleges. Once the acceptance was confirmed, as long as they didn't get into any trouble and graduated, they were good to go to college.

Before I got into college, all I had to consider was what I wanted to do in the future. Whom I wanted to become was my major consideration before the end of my high school years.

To be honest, I wasn't very old when I was about to graduate high school. I couldn't understand my true dream. Understanding what they really want to do is hard even to older people.

Still, interestingly, I could get a hint of what I wanted to do by seeing two small creatures. Before graduating from high school, I spent my time wandering around school, wanting to cherish the memories of high school life as I was about to leave. The central lake at our school was the place I frequented the most during my last days in high school. Many interesting things happened there.

It was on a weekend when there were no classes. I happened to stay alone at school. The school looked just like any other day, except for the fact that there was no one else around. Near our school's lake, there was a small café. It seemed like they served coffee, but I wasn't much of a coffee person. I never really ordered from there. I couldn't even recall if it was a café for sure.

I usually grabbed muffins there. They were reasonably priced. They served as a good snack when I felt hungry. So, buying a muffin and taking a walk near the lake became my routine when I was bored.

However, since it was the weekend, the café was closed. Nonetheless, there were plenty of chairs outside the café building.

I always used to sit there and gaze at the lake with a vacant mind. The lake at my school didn't have fish, so it was always a tranquil place. Right behind it, a small river flowed, but I didn't visit there often. It wasn't as well-maintained as our school's lake. I recall an incident where an alligator suddenly popped up there. I was glad that it didn't pop up in the lake.

Sitting by the lake, I could feel the heat rising from the sun. It almost felt like my cheeks were burning. As my face grew warmer, I'd start to feel like I had turned into a giant matchstick. So, whenever I found myself lost in thought, and my cheeks began to feel hot, I'd make my way back to the dormitory. That was my way of enjoying some rest.

Suddenly, I spotted a turtle and a duck. At my school, there were ducks and turtles that had settled in our school's lake. I wasn't sure if they were wild animals or not. I hadn't seen anyone taking care of them. So, maybe they were just wild animals without an owner. Yet, they acted like they owned the lake. If the police had seen them, they could have been arrested for trespassing. But they held more power in that lake than anyone I knew. They could even shoo away the principal if they wanted to. So, everyone just let them have the lake.

On that particular day, I saw the duck riding on the turtle's back. It seemed like the turtle didn't mind that arrangement. They continued moving around like that, with the duck comfortably perched on the turtle's back.

I found it incredibly fascinating. They seemed like friends, even though they were different species. Of course, it could have been a coincidence that the duck ended up on the turtle's back. But it seemed like the turtle had no intention of letting the duck down for quite a while.

After watching them for a while, I got up to head back to the dormitory. It was only then that the duck noticed my presence and hopped off the turtle's back. But what was even more astonishing was what happened after the duck dismounted. The turtle, as soon as the duck climbed down, started walking somewhere. What was really strange was that the duck began to follow the turtle as it walked, matching the turtle's pace perfectly. I watched in awe. It really seemed like they were friends.

I still think about the duck and the turtle occasionally. The image of the duck happily walking alongside the turtle at the turtle's slow pace was something that sticks with me. If I were to be reborn as a duck, I would want to be the duck that walks with the turtle. And if I were reborn as a turtle, I'd want to be the turtle that carries the duck and walks. Even if I weren't reborn as a duck or a turtle, I think I'd want to be their friend. Maybe that was my dream all along? I wanted to be someone who could walk alongside my friend, no matter who or what they were.

Then, while I was finishing my life as a high school student, I received a message from a university. It was an offer to pursue an academic degree at their institution. I told them that if it gave me the opportunity, I would do my best. In response, the university congratulated me. That's how I decided which university to attend.

CHAPTER 9

● ● ● ● ● ● ● ● ●

When I had to leave high school, I felt quite melancholic. It was the moment of parting ways with the friends I had just made. Nevertheless, I knew I had to change over time. As much as there were friends I was saying goodbye to, there were also new friends to meet.

Upon arriving at college for the first time, I was overwhelmed. The biggest building I had seen in the United States was the three-story office of the high school principal. During my time in the U.S., I hardly ventured outside of school. So, to me, the country was nothing more and nothing less than the high school I attended.

However, upon reaching the college campus, I was taken aback by the sheer size of the dormitories. These dorms were densely packed together, blocking my view in every direction. Apart from the clouds above, all I could see were dormitories. It felt like the country I had come to for my studies was quite vast.

"College is indeed different," I thought.

During my meeting with the dormitory supervisor, I was surprised to learn that the dormitory complex I had stayed in was just a small part of the university. In reality, countless dormitory and class complexes like the one I stayed in came together to make up the entire university. I had never imagined such a large-scale university before. Yet, as I thought more about it, perhaps even the university wasn't as vast as I once believed. After all, I knew that there were tens of thousands of universities worldwide. So, in comparison to an undiscovered world, my university might be considered relatively small.

With Earth being such a vast place, I couldn't help but wonder what a world ten times its size would be like. The only thing that came to mind was that real estate prices might have been ten times cheaper.

College was definitely different from high school. I had been a diligent student during high school, but when I entered college, I realized that I had to work twice as hard as I did in high school.

Initially, when I applied to college, I felt that once I got accepted, I could handle anything. However, things changed after I actually started attending college. I realized that most universities didn't teach classes with the aim of making students feel comfortable. They applied as much academic pressure as possible. Our university, in particular, was known for its strong academic rigor. So, I had to put in my best efforts.

I had many worries when I first came to college. I was afraid I wouldn't make any friends because I was quite shy around people I didn't know. I had difficulty speaking in front of strangers.

Fortunately, all these problems were solved as soon as I started to go to church. One of my friends I met in the dormitory introduced me to a church with a Korean pastor. When I first went to the church, the pastor and friends in the church welcomed me warmly. They made me feel comfortable. I continued to be close to them from before I went to the military until after I came back.

I wasn't someone who easily made friends even when I came to college. People often say that those with high IQs are smart. However, I believed that being good at communicating with others was also a wonderful talent. I often told people that those who were good at speaking seem very intelligent to me. Different people might have different directions in which they excel. Perhaps we all had undiscovered talents within us. Maybe life was a journey to discover our own potential. Maybe the God left some hidden talent within people and called it hope.

I wanted to become confident in front of people. I trembled like a criminal being interrogated by a police officer whenever I had to talk to unfamiliar people. I wanted to know how to fix this habit. I wondered if there was some kind of magical potion being sold at a vending machine.

Despite my odd behavior, the people who accepted me were my friends from church. I got to know them through a friend with the nickname "Grandpa."

When I was a freshman, I became friends with someone named Grandpa. He was just one year older than me but seemed much more mature. However, because he seemed too mature for his age, my friends used to tease him by calling him Grandpa. He was a friend who often needed rest as he found physical activities quite tiring. Thus, everyone agreed that the nickname perfectly fit him. Even Grandpa, who didn't like the nickname, couldn't raise an objection.

I first met Grandpa while I was on the school bus. I was never really interested in fashion, but since it was my first year at the school, I tried to look somewhat stylish. I didn't want to appear foolish in case I could make friends. Unfortunately, it seems I still looked foolish despite my efforts. The "stylish" outfit I wore consisted of a thick long-sleeved shirt and long pants. My idea of stylish clothing was more like something someone wouldn't wear for sports. I preferred comfortable clothes and often wore tracksuits. So, I didn't even have a clue about what kind of clothes to wear in everyday situations.

My first days in college were during a scorching summer. Wearing thick long-sleeved shirts and long pants made me feel like I was being roasted in an oven. I was a piece of roasted pork on the bus. However, there was only one thing I could do. That was to grumble about it.

"I should have worn different clothes," I said as I grumbled. That's when Grandpa caught my eye. He was on the same bus as me. I didn't know it at the time, but Grandpa overheard me grumbling. So, he thought I was a strange person and avoided talking to me. He found it odd that someone would wear thick clothes and complain about it on a hot summer day.

Grandpa was also a Korean, just like me. Meeting another Korean in an American university wasn't a common occurrence. There aren't that many Koreans in the United States. So, when Koreans met each other, they often greeted each other. However, it seems Grandpa wanted to keep his distance from me after seeing my attire and hearing my words. There had to be a reason why Grandpa was known for being wise.

When Grandpa was on the bus, he initially tried not to talk to me. However, I noticed that he was Korean. I greeted him warmly. I couldn't tell right away that he was Korean from the start. But I heard him conversing with another Korean sitting next to him in Korean. That's how I figured out that Grandpa was also Korean.

Grandpa couldn't resist engaging with someone who was friendly. So, we exchanged greetings and had a few conversations. I was really delighted to meet another Korean in college. I wasn't sure if I could navigate college life successfully.

That's why I wanted to make as many Korean friends as possible. Koreans are good at communication. Our lifestyles and cultures are similar, making it easy to become friends. Having more friends meant I could gather information about the university. That's why I didn't want to miss the chance to connect with Grandpa on the bus. I needed to graduate safely from this school. So, information like "Professors who give out A grades" was crucial. Friends often shared such information.

However, as I mentioned before, he didn't want to get too close to me. Frankly, I wasn't exactly a normal person. So, Grandpa didn't even share his contact information with me. Instead, we parted ways on the bus. In his own words, he didn't give me his contact information because he thought I was a strange person. However, luckily, our dorm rooms were right next to each other, so Grandpa and I became close friends. I didn't know how such a coincidence happened.

Fortunately, after we became close, Grandpa cleared up the misunderstanding that he had about me being strange. He became such a close friend that he honestly confessed that he thought I was strange in the past because of my clothing. He said I didn't seem like a bad person, at least. I was glad that Grandpa saw me in a positive light. I was sad that my fashion sense was that bad.

Grandpa introduced me to the church he attended. Since then, I really got into the life within the church. His influence played a big role in that. When my parents tried to take me to church back in South Korea, I used to run away every time. I'd spend the money they gave me for tithing on arcade games. But when Grandpa introduced me to the church, I was more willing to go along. I really liked the sermon of the pastor. Moreover, his wife served curry after every sermon. She just knew how to make perfect curry. That's why I never missed church every Sunday. And there was a pretty girl in the church, but I wouldn't say that I went diligently because of her. That would make me sound too needy.

And there, I could meet his church friends. Our church was a fantastic place with many great friends. So, after entering college, I almost exclusively hung out with my church friends. However, after completing my freshman year of college while hanging out with my church friends, a major challenge awaited me. I had to go to the military.

In South Korea, all males are required to serve in the military. Nowadays, it's about 18 months, but during my time, it was a bit longer. Typically, I had to serve around 21 months as a regular conscript. Special units like the Air Force had a longer service period. It was 24 months for them. And the Air Force was precisely where I served my military duty.

The military service wasn't as tough as anyone might expect. Honestly, it was tough, but there's no way to truly convey how tough it was at the time. Even though there were really tough moments, it's something that people who haven't been in the military might not fully understand. For example, in the military, we had chemical, biological, radiological, and nuclear (CBRN) training. It was training to prepare us for chemical, biological, or radiological attacks. It was simple training. All I had to do was enter a room full of CBRN gas. Since it was harmless gas made only for training, no one was injured. Still, it involved enduring intense pain for a few minutes. I've often heard people in movies say they feel like dying after a breakup. But if they had a chance to go through CBRN training, their perspective could change. Feeling like I was about to die is really, really painful. People could physically die.

So, I didn't feel confident describing my military experiences. That's why I would say that the military wasn't as tough as anyone might think. Unless someone experiences it firsthand, he couldn't truly understand how tough it is. I just want to show some respect to those protecting the peace.

Nevertheless, I completed my military service without any

major issues. (Well, there were some issues, but I won't describe them, because they were actually major issues, mostly caused by me.)

The two years eventually passed by. The military service period that seemed endless while I was in it eventually came to an end. I returned to college to continue my studies. I was looking forward to reuniting with my friends.

However, when I came back, I discovered something new. There was a new addition to our friend group. Her name was Sara.

Sara was a very positive and energetic person. She always seemed to be bursting with energy. She was a living battery. She was a hardworking student who was also involved in military activities.

In the United States, people who wanted to earn money for college could enlist in the military. In that way, they could receive military training while attending school. The military or the government would then provide financial support for their education.

At our college, I could always hear someone shouting in the early morning, around 6 AM. It wasn't roosters; it was people starting their early morning. At first, I didn't know what those shouts were all about. Sara later explained that they were the sounds of military training. In the military, they used shouting to boost morale and motivation, especially in the morning. The reason Sara knew about these shouts was that she was in the military too. Her voice could be heard among those shouts.

However, Sara and I didn't become close right away. I had no idea how to talk to girls.

I first met Sara at my friend's dormitory. My church friends occasionally invited each other to our respective dorms. Our main source of entertainment was drinking beer or wine.

When I first returned from the military and met with my friends, I saw Sara there for the first time. I was taken aback. I felt a bit awkward around people I hadn't met before. I initially tried to treat Sara the way I treated my church friends, but it wasn't that easy. I couldn't shake off the uncomfortable feeling. She might have been aware of my discomfort. She was quite careful in her interactions with me. Still, it seemed like she didn't want to make me uncomfortable.

The funny thing was that even though I saw Sara every time I met with my friends, I never really got used to her. It didn't bother me when we were all together, but strangely, when it was just Sara and me, it felt awkward. So, when I was with her, I couldn't say anything and would just sit there silently. It was as if my brain stopped working when she was around.

Nonetheless, I tried to talk to her sometimes, even with a trembling voice. So, I asked her about her major courses and the personalities of her professors. I didn't know what kind of conversation she liked, but I felt that the atmosphere would become awkward if we stayed silent. I had to ask questions.

Sara answered those questions sincerely. She didn't show any reluctance, even if I repeated questions that might not have been appropriate for the situation. It felt like Sara understood that I wasn't great at conversing. If that's the case, she truly was a great person.

Surprisingly, we eventually became "Best Friends." The reason Sara and I became "Best Friends" was quite simple. There wasn't anything special about it. I just declared it out of the blue, and she accepted it.

The event that led to it happened at our college's Student Center. Our college had a library and a Student Center. The Student Center was a place created by the college for students to enjoy. It had rooms for band performances, comfortable chairs and TVs for entertainment, seating for studying, and rooms for hosting job-related events.

The main reason students visited the Student Center was for the dining options. There were many restaurants in the Student Center. The Student Center had a total of 3 floors, and each floor had its own restaurants. On the 1st floor, there was a fast-food joint, while the 2nd floor had Mediterranean, Japanese, Indian, and a salad bar. I usually dined on the 2nd floor. On the 3rd floor, there was a buffet that professors often frequented. It was quite upscale.

I enjoyed eating alone. After I grew up, I started to enjoy imagining different worlds once more. When I was alone, I could indulge in entertaining fantasies. I didn't like interruptions when my imagination was flowing. Once it was interrupted, I couldn't pick up where I left off. So, dining while enjoying the imaginative thoughts that popped into my head became my hobby.

Despite my preference for solitude, there were moments when I would encounter others. One of those moments was when I met Sara and my church friend Amy at the Student Center.

It happened when I was having my meal alone, as usual, engrossed in my childlike imagination. That's when Sara and Amy saw me and approached me. I was so lost in my imagination that I didn't even notice them coming. I realized they were there when they stood in front of me and called my name.

Seeing them made me genuinely happy, but I quickly felt embarrassed. When I'm alone, I often make silly expressions and talk to myself. I worried that Sara and Amy might have seen me acting that way.

When Sara and Amy approached, I greeted them warmly, exaggerating our familiarity as if I were someone who had been caught doing something wrong. Fortunately, Amy didn't seem to have any reservations. She had known me for quite some time, so she was already aware that I was a bit unusual.

The problem was Sara. Although we had met a few times, it

was still difficult to become close to her. I wondered how I had become close to Amy. Maybe if I approached Sara the same way I did with Amy, it would work. However, becoming close to Amy had happened a long time ago. I couldn't remember the exact process. So, I was stuck, not knowing how to become close to Sara.

Amy was quick to pick up on things. She seemed to notice that I felt awkward around Sara. So, she tried to facilitate our conversation.

"Do you know Sara, Hoon?" Amy asked. Amy had a talent for making conversations flow smoothly. With just that one sentence, the awkwardness between Sara and me lessened significantly. If someone were to sell the skill Amy had, I would buy it even on a subscription basis. A subscription always seemed too expensive regardless of the price. Still, I would buy it for something incredible.

I tried to answer Amy's question. I did know Sara, after all. So, I intended to say that I knew Sara. But for some reason, I became nervous and ended up exaggerating my response.

"Of course! Sara is my Best Friend!"

Sara and I had never really had a comfortable, casual conversation before. We hadn't shared any friendly, easygoing chats. Sara had the talent to make people around her have a good time. But I wasn't very good at brightening up the atmosphere like Sara was. Sometimes, I wasn't sure if Sara and I were even friends. Of course, given our history and the time we spent knowing each other, some could say we were friends. However, there were moments when the term "acquaintance" seemed more appropriate for our relationship. In many ways, our connection felt closer to that of acquaintances.

But suddenly, I had blurted out that Sara was my Best Friend. Paradoxically, it felt like an expression that emphasized the awkwardness between us. Typically, I wouldn't use "Best Friend" with someone I was still somewhat uncomfortable around.

I regretted saying that Sara was my Best Friend. I had made an exaggerated mistake for no reason. Sara also seemed puzzled by whether we truly were Best Friends or not.

I responded to my own blunder with a puzzled expression, "Oh, aren't we Best Friends?"

I was flustered and struggling to find my words. Looking back, even a simple response like "Yeah, she is," to Amy's question "Do you know Sara?" would have sufficed. Given that we weren't very close, I didn't need to proclaim her as my Best Friend.

I felt like I had made another mistake. My face reddened with embarrassment. Sara, Amy, and I were now stuck in an awkward silence. I was trying to salvage the situation, but I didn't know how. I was adding hesitant "uh..." sounds to the conversation, as my brain seemed to have run out of fuel. I had just eaten, but why was my brain running on empty?

However, quick-witted Sara suddenly started laughing, then said something unexpected.

"That's right! Hoon is my Best Friend!"

As a result of her confirmation, Sara and I became "Best Friends." Sara laughed heartily, even though I didn't quite understand what was so funny. But seeing her laugh, I started to forget about my mistake. Sara's laughter seemed to be telling me not to worry about a slip of the tongue. Friends always had each other's backs. Perhaps Sara was truly my friend after all.

I couldn't forget the momentary laughter Sara showed me. It was like an unforgettable fragrance. Sara left a fragrance with me. If such a fragrance could linger in the world for a long time, everyone could be happier.

I wished for only good things for Sara. She was undoubtedly someone who could leave good memories in anyone's heart. People who can make others happy must await a bright future.

The reason people strive to do good things even when life was tough was probably to witness such happy days.

I had a small wish. I hoped that both Sara and I would do well and, someday, we would meet each other with happy smiles. If that day came, I would surely be able to call her my Best Friend once more.

Still, such a day could never come. Not long after, Sara passed away.

'Acute Leukemia'

This disease can cause a person die within a few days. Strangely, it's not easy to diagnose. Thus, Sara lived her whole life without knowing that she had acute leukemia. By the time she found out what illness she had, she had only three days left with us. It was barely enough time to say her last goodbyes to her family.

Among my church friends, there was a girl named Jenny. She was Amy's roommate and had a really pleasant personality. Sara was very close to Jenny and Amy. It was only natural because Sara, Amy, and Jenny were all great people. Good people tend to get along well with each other. It was no exception in their case. So, when we went to Sara's funeral, Amy, Jenny, and a few other church friends were there with me.

On the way to Sara's funeral, Jenny said something. She mentioned that there were times when Sara became unusually sensitive. Sara was usually very easygoing, so when she suddenly acted sensitive, it took Jenny by surprise. But as it turned out, these mood swings were one of the symptoms of acute leukemia.

Sara had not been feeling well for a while, so she had gone to a nearby hospital for blood tests several times. However, the hospital always assured her that there was nothing wrong with her. As I mentioned, acute leukemia, the disease she had, was tricky because it could hide and then suddenly manifest itself.

Sara continued to suffer from the disease without anyone understanding her pain. Sara had many difficult moments. She often had nosebleeds and anemia. She would often faint, but nobody understood how difficult it was for Sara. Pain is most acute when no one understands the suffering.

I still remember the day I heard about Sara's death. It was the same day that was originally planned for all of us from the church to go on a trip.

At first, I couldn't accept Sara's death. I couldn't believe that Sara had passed away on the day we had planned to go on a trip with friends. But when I realized that Sara's death was a reality, tears welled up.

During the journey to the funeral, everything felt like a joke. Somehow, when we arrived, it felt like we would be at the condo we had planned to stay at for our trip. And Sara would be there, laughing and saying, "We got you!" I could have laughed and gone along with that kind of joke.

But the place the car arrived at was the funeral home. A hearse was waiting at the main entrance, with its unique appearance that I could instantly recognize. Sara had indeed passed away.

All my friends went inside the funeral home. I tried to follow them into the funeral home, but I couldn't pass through the main entrance. If I went inside the funeral home, it felt like Sara would really leave.

Before I knew it, everyone had gone inside the funeral home. I was the only one left at the main entrance. Shortly after, I heard that the funeral service would proceed soon. There was going to be a time to say a final farewell to Sara. Only then did I stand up from my spot and enter the funeral home.

Many people had gathered at the funeral home. There were also soldiers. They seemed like Sara's friends. Sara had to be active in the military as well. Surely they must have liked Sara as well. She was a friend they couldn't help but like.

As the funeral proceeded, Sara's father spoke about memories with Sara and made one request.

"If anyone has pictures taken with Sara, I would appreciate it if you could send them."

My friends and I wanted to send pictures of Sara. However, it was at that moment that I realized I didn't have many pictures with Sara.

After the funeral service, Sara had to be taken away in the hearse. But before that, everyone had a chance to say their final farewells to Sara, who lay in the casket. People took turns coming forward to offer their condolences to Sara's family and to say their goodbyes to Sara. They would greet her briefly and then step aside for the next person to do the same.

It was finally my turn to offer my condolences to Sara's family. Then, I approached the casket. The casket was elevated on a slightly raised platform. I couldn't see Sara's face until I stepped onto the platform. When I got on the platform, I saw Sara lying in the casket. It was clear that she had truly passed away. Sara had such a peaceful expression. It felt like if I said something, she would call my name again.

I glanced back for a moment. Everyone had such sorrowful expressions. It was strange. Sara lay so peacefully, and yet they were all so sad. It was as if death resided not in Sara but within the grieving people.

I approached Sara and whispered softly, "Hey, Best Friend."

Whenever I called her that, Sara would always respond with, "Hello, Best Friend!"

But for some reason, Sara didn't respond.

When I saw Sara off, I could see Sara's face through her portrait photo. In the portrait photo, Sara was smiling brightly. However, for some reason, it seemed like Sara was very sad. I felt like I was about to cry. Sara always seemed happy whenever we greeted each other. Even when we exchanged our final farewells at the funeral, Sara seemed carefree. But why did Sara in the portrait photo appear to be crying so sadly? She was clearly smiling.

I saw a young boy for a moment, holding the portrait photo. I had never seen him before, but he had a look of despair on his face. It wasn't a sad expression, but rather a face that didn't know how to come to terms with reality.

I had a gut feeling that the boy was a member of Sara's family. Only a family member would be so devastated. Moreover, it was unlikely that he would be holding the portrait photo if he wasn't family. He looked slightly younger than Sara, so he must have been her little brother. He seemed sadder than anyone else at the funeral.

Sara's brother wasn't shedding tears, but he looked incredibly sad. I knew why he wasn't crying. Sometimes, in truly sad moments, tears don't come. Ironically, people sometimes cry when they're happy. Tears might not always represent sadness.

After Sara's passing, when the weekend came, I went to church. I wasn't someone who prayed regularly. I occasionally offered stupid prayers, mostly asking for a bit of luck when I had to guess answers on an exam question. But on that day, I had something I wanted to pray for. It was a simple prayer, asking God to let Sara go to heaven. I hadn't known Sara for very long, but I genuinely believed she was a good person. So, I prayed that she would find a good place in the afterlife.

People wished to go to heaven. However, no one really wished to face death themselves. Perhaps those who wished to go to heaven were hoping to find one during their lifetime.

If there was a heaven in the world, what would it look like? I wasn't sure where heaven was, but I would call where Sara was heaven. She gave me a place where I wanted to belong.

The summer vacation arrived not long after. I was becoming a senior, with graduation approaching. A year ago, I applied for an internship position in a research lab during the summer vacation and got accepted. But the summer became the time that I went to meet Mr. Buffett.

Grandpa had recommended the research lab to me. It was run by a very promising professor at a university. He had recommended me to join his research lab.

I had been preparing to join that lab for several years. I liked the professor. I liked his interview style. He was quite unique. When I first went to greet him, which was a year before the summer I went to meet Mr. Buffett, he asked me to introduce myself. I answered diligently. Then, I told him that I wanted to join his research lab. However, his response was rather indifferent.

"I see."

That was the only thing he said. Then he told me that I didn't need to come to his research lab.

I really wanted to join his research lab, so I wanted to show more of my passion. However, the professor didn't give me any more opportunities to speak. I thought I had been rejected during the interview. To get into a university's research lab, I needed the professor to approve me to join. However, the professor didn't tell me that I had been accepted. He didn't seem particularly interested in me.

However, the professor asked me a question. "What's your dream?" I hesitated at his question. It was the first time someone had asked me about my dream face-to-face. I hadn't really had a specific dream; I had simply learned from a young age that I needed to become an outstanding person. I had learned that I had to be someone recognized by others. So, even though I didn't really have one, I shared the dream that had come to me.

"I've seen the top 10 most famous people in history before. People like Jesus and Napoleon. I want to become one of them."

The professor listened to my story and then looked at me for a moment. Suddenly, he asked another question, "Napoleon, huh? Did you happen to leave out Genghis Khan?"

I shared what I remembered, saying, "I remember Genghis Khan was ranked fourth."

The professor started laughing when he heard this story. Then, he added some encouraging words, "When people dream, at least half of it tends to come true."

He looked at me and continued, "I like you. If you want, you can intern at our research lab during the university summer break. And when you graduate from college, you can come to our lab as a graduate student."

That was the outcome of the interview I had with him.

The people who went to that professor's research lab often published their papers in prestigious journals. Additionally, after graduating from that lab, most of them went on to become professors at good universities. Going to that professor's research lab held a special significance because of these reasons.

However, I didn't go to that professor's research lab. Instead, I went to meet Mr. Buffett during that summer break. Summer break held a special meaning for college students. It was a time to gain experiences that would benefit their future.

I had the opportunity to go to the research lab. It seemed like a great opportunity to join the professor's lab where I had interviewed. Under his guidance, I felt I could become an outstanding person.

However, when Sara passed away, memories of the past resurfaced. It was a time when I had contemplated leaving the world myself.

I was unpopular as a child. Once, simply for riding the same elevator, I was dragged by bullies to an alley and beaten until my face turned pale. The world was a tough place for me.

I once went to an academy. One of my relatives attended the same academy as me. I didn't want my relatives to know about my bad reputation. So, I tried not to cause trouble at the academy.

But one day, an accident suddenly occurred. A certain child tried to play a prank on me. He was a kid who had never spoke to me before. He simply disliked the fact that I was in the same class as him. So, when I tried to enter the classroom at the academy, he closed the door from the inside. The problem was that my finger got caught in the door gap. I tried with all my might to pull my finger out of the door. But I couldn't open the door at all. I screamed for them to open the door and let me out. But the kid inside only tried to close the door even harder. Laughter was heard from inside the door. There were more than one person pulling the door. I screamed and begged the kids inside to open the door. Still, they didn't listen.

I was in terrible pain. Still, I was engulfed in terror more than pain. I couldn't express it in words, but I was truly scared. What scared me the most wasn't the fact that my finger was being crushed. It was the realization that no matter how much I begged, the kids wouldn't open the door for me. The idea that my pleading was meaningless was truly terrifying.

The commotion lasted for a while. It was only when the kids inside the door were exhausted from pulling that they finally opened it. As I pulled my hand out from between the door, I saw something small fall. It was my fingernail. But I couldn't even pay attention to my fingernail. I was in a panic. I ran back and forth in the hallway for a while. I didn't even think about going to find a teacher. I was like a baby, screaming and running around, unable to do anything else. People really become like babies in truly terrifying moments.

When I recall that moment, I don't remember how much my

finger hurt. I just remember blood in the hallway and thinking, "Is this all my blood?" and "Could there really be this much blood from a person?"

As I continued to cause a commotion, the teacher soon came to find me. I didn't hear a word the teacher said. Even when the teacher called my name, I just kept running around. Eventually, the teacher started grabbing my arm and pulling me. Only then did I realize that the teacher had come. I sniffled and followed the teacher.

In the same building where the academy was located, there was a hospital. The teacher took me to that hospital. Shortly afterward, I was taken into the operating room, and the doctor began to suture my finger. I finally felt relieved when the doctor applied anesthesia on my wound. I finally became calm. It was funny to remember that moment. I couldn't remember how much it hurt when my finger was being crushed, but I could remember my heart beating when the anesthesia was applied.

After the accident, something strange happened. I found myself in a situation where I had to leave the academy. I returned to the academy after the incident, but what I wished for wasn't anything special. I just wanted to hear assurances that the same thing wouldn't happen again from the kids who hurt me. I didn't hold any grudges against them. I didn't think they hurt me out of malice. I believed that their prank accidently caused a huge problem. I just hoped that what happened back then wouldn't happen again.

However, the way I was treated at the academy was strange. The kids who hurt me started avoiding me. Suddenly, I became a liability to them. They became uncomfortable around me, as if they had become the ones who hurt me. So, I requested to leave the academy.

The funny thing was that even the teachers at the academy requested me to leave. To them, I was just another student. However, there were quite a few students who either hurt me or associated with those who did. From the teachers' perspective, my leaving was a better deal than their leaving the academy. So, eventually, I ended up leaving the academy without receiving any apology.

When such incidents occurred, I found it really tough. The hardest moments were when I couldn't show my distress. I couldn't let my friends see that I was hurting. No matter what happened to me, people hoped I would quietly overcome it. They said it was a way to become a good person. But why wasn't I allowed to struggle, even though I, too, had difficult moments?

At one point when I was feeling extremely overwhelmed, there was a time when I contemplated making a bad choice. Unknowingly, I searched online for ways people could die. It's said that there are veins and arteries in a person's wrist. Veins are the visible blood vessels on our wrists. Cutting these veins causes bleeding initially, but soon it stops. However, it's said that in order for a person to die, one must cut the arteries located deeper, beyond what's visible to the naked eye.

I once took a knife and brought it to my wrist. Initially, I thought it was a crazy act. However, as the difficult times repeated, the frequency of bringing the knife to my wrist increased. I could feel a shift in my consciousness regarding my actions. Initially, I thought dying from mere sadness was silly. But as time passed, I couldn't find a reason not to die. When I first brought the knife to my wrist, I unconsciously felt the instinct to pull it away. But as time went on, I felt the anger wanting to push the knife into my wrist.

Eventually, I wanted to seek revenge on those who made me suffer. I wanted to show those who didn't understand my pain how angry I was. So, ending my life felt like my duty. I thought that seeing myself dead would show those who tormented me how much I had suffered.

I didn't want to hate others. Life was too precious to live while harboring hatred. However, I was getting tired. Living this life was becoming increasingly difficult.

I once heard a story about life being like a marathon, shared by someone offering life lessons. Some people emphasized that life is not a sprint but a continuous run, much like a marathon. They said I had to keep running to win the race.

However, I couldn't figure out where I was running to. What was I running for? People always told me not to ask such questions. They said questions should be asked after reaching the destination. But how could I reach a destination if I didn't know where I was heading? Did the person who imparted the lesson about life being a marathon know where the destination was? Was he on his way to his desired destination? I couldn't discern whether life was a marathon or a short race. All I wished for was that when I stopped running, there would be someone by my side welcoming me and loving me.

When I felt like there was going to be no one near me at the end of my life, I felt no need to continue it. That's when I wanted to end it.

But there was someone who showed me the purpose of life. It was my elementary school teacher, Teacher Song. His teachings helped me avoid making wrong choices.

CHAPTER 10

● ● ● ● ● ● ● ● ● ●

My last elementary school was a highly competitive place. Students were extremely driven to become the best. They spent more than half of their day at their desks. They were like living computers.

At that elementary school, there was a teacher who became my last homeroom teacher. That was Teacher Song, because his last name was Song. It was memorable because it was a last name I hadn't encountered before.

Teacher Song was quite unique. Even his appearance stood out from others. Teacher Song had arms as strong as baseball bats. I always thought that people's arms were supposed to be soft and squishy. If someone poked my arms, they'd go "boing." However, if someone touched Teacher Song's arms, it felt like they'd go "thud."

Teacher Song's way of thinking was reminiscent of a firefighter. He was always ready to take action, much like fire trucks that didn't stop for red lights. Once he had a goal in mind, there was no halting his determination. Teacher Song had a very distinct teaching style that he firmly believed in. Even if it diverged from conventional methods, he would confidently implement his approach.

One of Teacher Song's notable teaching methods involved playing soccer on rainy days, sometimes even during usual classes. When he noticed rain during a lesson, Teacher Song would take the students to the soccer field and engage in a game with them.

Before I met Teacher Song, I had never played sports in my life. Moreover, I had never even attempted sports on rainy days. On rainy days, I didn't exercise at home either. The gloomy weather sapped my motivation. However, when Teacher Song saw rain, he would grab the kids and rush out to the soccer field. He made us run and play until we forgot about the cold. What was fascinating was that during those moments, all the kids would run around like they were crazy. They didn't even realize how much time had passed; they just enjoyed exercising. Even the girls would come in with rough tackles. Watching them, it felt like the Vikings had finally invaded Asia.

The turning point that led to my close relationship with Teacher Song was his hobby, which was reading English books to students. Our school had one hour of self-study time within the school each week, during which the homeroom teacher could teach students whatever they wanted.

Teacher Song used that time to read us the book "Holes." It was a very interesting book. I was so engaged that I didn't feel sleepy for the first time while listening to the teacher. When I listened to Teacher Song's storytelling, it was impossible for me to fall asleep. His reading was as exciting as a rock concert. I was almost tempted to dye my hair red and put on heavy black eyeliner around my eyes.

Teacher Song read the English book "Holes" to us, translating it line by line into Korean. Reading an English book to students wasn't an easy task, but Teacher Song had a strong attachment to his students. That's why he chose to eventually read the entire English book to us.

I loved Teacher Song's storytelling, so I would often help move "Holes" book from his office to my classroom. Teacher Song also trusted me with the book because he knew I was the most focused when it came to the story.

Sometimes, when I looked at the book while moving it, I could see that it was well-worn. Teacher Song had read the book dozens of times to translate it into Korean for the students. He painstakingly looked up and wrote down the meanings of unfamiliar words and grammar in the book. Teacher Song's dedication to the book was a testament to his love for his students.

I was known as the student who often got into trouble with other students during that time. Our school was quite closed-off, with mostly elite students. In contrast, I was a country kid from a rural area, so I had trouble adapting to the school environment.

During a period when I was struggling with a lot, Teacher Song called me out. He would occasionally call me out and make me exercise or do some work when he saw that I was feeling down. Teacher Song's saying was that a healthy body leads to a healthy mind. He believed that doing something was better than doing nothing in any situation.

Teacher Song asked me if I had any dreams or aspirations for the future. He was the first person in my life to inquire about my dreams.

However, I didn't know what my dream was. I had never dreamed in my life. All I ever wished for was to go home as soon as possible and sleep for an extra hour. I didn't have many other aspirations. I had never really hoped for my life to improve.

I honestly told Teacher Song that I didn't have a dream. In response, Teacher Song spoke to me very seriously, urging me to think about my dreams. He asked me to tell him about my dream within the next few days.

I had never thought about dreams before. I didn't even know what a dream was. I had never heard about people's desires or wishes being fulfilled. Nevertheless, I decided to follow Teacher Song's guidance. I was a student who listened well to Teacher Song's words. So, I created a dream as per his instructions before he called me again.

Unfortunately, a few days weren't enough time for me to come up with a dream that I really desired. Thus, I just came up with a dream that sounded nice. When Teacher Song asked me what my dream was, I told him that my dream was to become a doctor, as people often praised doctors as great professionals. Teacher Song praised me, saying that the dream would become a source of energy in my life. Still, Teacher Song had one last thing to share with me. He said that no matter what dream I had, I should always aim to be the best at it. So, my dream was decided: to become the world's greatest doctor.

I couldn't understand why Teacher Song had such high expectations for me. I wasn't an outstanding student at school. Becoming a doctor wasn't something anyone could achieve just by having a dream; it was a profession for the most exceptional individuals in the country.

However, Teacher Song told me that I could do anything. I couldn't understand what that meant at the time. I simply felt good because Teacher Song seemed to believe in me.

I couldn't know if Teacher Song was right. In reality, I didn't become a doctor. I had never actually aimed to become a doctor. My goal was simply to find a well-paying job, no matter what it was.

It wasn't until I got much older that I felt like I understood why Teacher Song had told me to have dreams. Teacher Song wanted me to trust myself. Thus, until I could do so, he wanted to be the one who trusted me. I tried to understand why he cared about me so much. I realized that he tried to trust me because he loved me. Believing in someone meant loving him, I guess.

In my toughest moments, someone's belief in me became a great source of strength for me. Thinking about Teacher Song's choice to believe in me, I couldn't give up trusting myself. He didn't teach me why I shouldn't die, but he taught me that I was the one who was loved.

I was grateful to Teacher Song. That's why I couldn't give up on life. I felt like if I disappeared, people like Teacher Song who loved me would feel empty. So instead of choosing to die, I wanted to show them someday that I had become a better person.

I've heard an interesting experiment story from the past. It was an experiment to find out whom people were attracted to. In this experiment, participants provided their photos to a research institution. The institution then created new photos by changing only the gender based on the received pictures. They mixed these newly created photos with pictures of other people and showed them to the participants. The research institution asked the participants to choose who they would want to date.

Interestingly, the majority of the participants expressed a desire to date the person in the photos that looked like themselves with only the gender changed.

At first, I thought that people wanted to date someone familiar. But now, things seem to have changed a bit. I felt like people just wanted to love themselves. Perhaps, we all wanted to.

Someday, if the day comes when I can love myself, I want to meet Teacher Song again. And when I can, I want to say that I've become someone who can love myself. Somehow, it felt like the best thank-you I could offer him. I pray that day will come someday.

After coming to Omaha, one thing happened to me. That was writing a letter. I became anxious the moment I arrived in Omaha, thinking about meeting Mr. Buffett. I didn't know what to say to him. But then I suddenly wanted to do something. That was giving Mr. Buffett a gift. I had heard about what Mr. Buffett had done for others, but I had not heard about what gifts he had received. I wanted to do something he would like.

He was one of the people who made it possible for me to dream. So, when I met him, I wanted to thank him for giving me a chance to become a better person. I wondered what I should give him as a gift. Then, I suddenly remembered that Mr. Buffett enjoys reading. He spent most of his day reading. So, I wanted to write him a letter with a story that he would enjoy reading. Thus, I started writing a letter containing stories that no one had heard. These stories were none other than the stories contained in this book. This book was ultimately just a more elaborate version of the letter I wrote for Mr. Buffett.

Writing about past experiences in the letter was a painful task. Facing my pain once again made it feel like the agony of that time was resurfacing. I even questioned if I should have written the letter at all. However, as I continued to write the letter, something mysterious happened. I could feel a change happening within me. For some reason, the fear and pain of the past didn't weigh as heavily on me as before.

What changed? Could it be that I've always feared the past because I've been trying to escape from it? It felt like I was liberated from my past fears. It was a new feeling. I felt like I was free from the curse that had tormented me. Now, I seemed to be able to accept even the parts of myself that I hadn't liked before, little by little. Did I try to meet Mr. Buffett for this moment?

My desire to meet Mr. Buffett and the dream of becoming someone like him wasn't driven by any special reason. It was simply my heart responding to the words of encouragement from Teacher Song, who told me to dream. Somehow, when he believed in me, I felt like I could achieve my dreams.

He told me to dream the world's greatest dream. So when I thought about wanting to meet Mr. Buffett, I didn't hesitate to meet him. I wanted to be like Mr. Buffett. I wondered why I had such a dream. what was it about me that led me to dream such a dream?

In the world, it's often said that many things are required for success. Some say you need capital, others argue that skills are the most crucial. Some believe luck is the key to success. However, looking back now, what made me challenge my dreams and believe that I could achieve them was simply one person who believed in me. Perhaps what's truly needed to fulfill dreams is someone who believes in and loves me. If that's really the case, dreaming should be truly wonderful.

I went to meet Mr. Buffett about a year after Sara passed away. It was a sudden thought, the desire to meet him, that came to me. The next day, I found myself heading to Omaha, where Mr. Buffett's company, Berkshire Hathaway, was located, to meet him.

Omaha was a city that felt like it was still holding onto its peace. Driving along the highway, I could see vast prairies stretching out right beside me, occasionally spotting horses running freely. Just watching those horses run without any restraints made me feel better.

I stayed at a place hosted by a person named Ryan, whom I found on Airbnb. Airbnb was a platform that allowed regular people to rent out their homes to others. Ryan's place was not a hotel, but I could book and stay there nonetheless.

Ryan's place was quite far from Mr. Buffett's company. It wasn't walkable. Even taking public transportation took quite a while. The sun that had been directly overhead when I went to Mr. Buffett's company had moved toward the horizon by the time I returned.

The reason Mr. Buffett's company was far from Ryan's house was simple. I didn't have much money at the time, so I had to find the cheapest boarding house. There were no affordable boarding houses near Mr. Buffett's company. Thus, I had to stay at Ryan's house even though it was quite far away. Fortunately, I liked Ryan and his house, so I was comfortable during my stay in Omaha.

As I planned, I started to clean the streets near Mr. Buffett's company. It was my own plan to meet Mr. Buffett. I purchased cleaning supplies near Mr. Buffett's company. I had previously researched and found a market where I could buy cleaning tools. I bought a broom that was slightly smaller than my height. The broom had green bristles and a wooden handle. The green bristles looked exceptionally clean. I felt that with this broom, I could make anything clean when I swept with it.

If I were a bit older and had more money, I would have wanted to meet Mr. Buffett in a different way, namely by having lunch with him. Mr. Buffett used to auction off the privilege of having lunch with him, and all the money raised from the auction went to charity.

To meet him in this way, people typically needed several million to tens of millions of dollars. Some individuals have spent as much as $4 million to have a meal with Mr. Buffett. I didn't have anywhere near that amount of money. I had earned some money over the years through military service, but it was nowhere near the required amount. I earned $2,000 in two years in the military. I would have had to work in the military from the time Jesus was born, which was 2,000 years ago, to earn $4 million at that rate.

So, I couldn't have the opportunity to meet Mr. Buffett over lunch in that manner. However, I wasn't too disappointed. Someday, when I become a truly remarkable person, I would like to come back and ask him to have lunch with me. I might have to win the auction. Still, I would also be happy to win it, since the cost would be worth the price. Mr. Buffett was someone worth dreaming about.

In Omaha, I woke up early every morning, headed to Mr. Buffett's company for cleaning, and then returned home. That was my daily routine in Omaha. I had no way of knowing exactly when or how I might have the opportunity to meet Mr. Buffett. I couldn't even be certain that I would meet him at all. Nevertheless, I continued going to Mr. Buffett's company for cleaning every morning and returned home when the sky darkened.

One day, as I was returning from Mr. Buffett's company, it was getting quite late. On such evenings, taking the bus made me nervous. I was traveling alone in Omaha. I felt like I might encounter some kind of trouble or stranger on the way back to Ryan's house from the bus station. I had to walk for a long time to reach Ryan's house after getting off at the bus stop. Being alone made it difficult to ask for help if I found myself in a difficult situation. So, I decided to use Uber instead of the bus.

In the Uber, I met a driver who liked to fish a lot. His car was filled with fishing gear. There was a distinct fishy smell in the car. It appeared that he devoted a lot of time to fishing.

He greeted me as soon as he saw me.

"Hello?"

I smiled and replied to his greeting.

"Hello."

We were riding in the Uber for a while. I was actually a bit uncomfortable to sit next to him. I had sweated a lot while cleaning, so I thought I might have an odor. I could only hope that the unpleasant smell from my body wouldn't reach his nose.

However, he didn't seem to be too concerned about my smell. Honestly, he had quite a strong smell himself, specifically a fishy odor. It seemed like he had just been fishing. It was fortunate that my smell didn't make him unpleasant.

We were riding in the taxi for a while. Then, he suddenly struck up a conversation.

"Is that a broom?"

He pointed at the broom I was holding. I had the broom with me that I had used for cleaning the streets.

I replied to him, "Yes, that's right."

He asked, "Where are you taking it? What do you need it for?"

After hesitating for a moment when he asked again, I answered honestly, "I used it for cleaning around Mr. Buffett's company."

He looked somewhat surprised and began to inquire, "Were you working at Mr. Buffett's company?"

I firmly replied that I had never worked there, saying, "No, I have no connection with Mr. Buffett. I just wanted to clean his company once, that's all."

I responded and then fell silent for a moment. Upon reflection, it seemed quite awkward to clean Mr. Buffett's company, since I never knew him. However, before I could dwell on my embarrassment, he asked me, "Why did you want to clean it?"

I hesitated for a moment before responding, "I was curious if I might accidentally meet him."

In response to my answer, he replied with a cheerful tone, "So you came here to try to meet Mr. Buffett too? I met him once before; it was truly a special experience."

I looked at him in surprise and asked, "Have you ever met Mr. Buffett?"

He said, "A long time ago, I bought a book about him and went to find him. I wanted to get his autograph. Surprisingly, I was able to meet him and get his autograph. It was quite easy to meet him back then. But it's been a while, so I don't know if he still grants such requests."

I suddenly learned a way to meet Mr. Buffett from him. However, I wasn't sure if I could actually meet him, just as he had done. As he mentioned, he had met Mr. Buffett a long time ago. I wasn't sure if Mr. Buffett would still meet with people who wanted to meet him.

Thus, I decided to visit Mr. Buffett's company briefly and inquire with someone around the company if I could actually meet Mr. Buffett.

By the time I was in the Uber, it was already evening. I was on my way back to the Airbnb where I was staying. I decided to proceed with my new plan the next day. The next day, I learned that I couldn't meet Mr. Buffett.

As morning broke, I headed out to the street I had been cleaning for weeks. On that day, I didn't bring the broom with me. I just wanted to check if I could meet Mr. Buffett.

By the time I arrived at Mr. Buffett's company, it was already past the the start of office hours. It was a lunchtime. The street was most crowded during the morning rush hour, but there were fewer people right after that. Thus, I couldn't find anyone suitable to ask about meeting Mr. Buffett around his company.

Fortunately, I saw three people entering Mr. Buffett's company. They were carrying sandwiches in one hand and had employee badges with their names hanging around their necks.

I approached them and asked, "Is this where Mr. Buffett works?"

One of them nodded and said, "Yes, he works upstairs."

I couldn't help but let out a momentary exclamation. It felt like I had just seen the actual space where Mr. Buffett worked. Until then, the company felt like one of millions of buildings I had seen before. But now, it was one of a kind.

However, I accidentally got caught up in my amazement and failed to ask the more important question. I wanted to inquire if Mr. Buffett accepted meetings from strangers like me. However, while I was in awe, they entered the company building.

I hesitated for a moment and waited for other people to come, hoping to ask them. However, there were no people coming in or out of Mr. Buffett's company. The main entrance of Mr. Buffett's company stood still like a rock in a quiet forest.

I was curious if the people like those I had just encountered might be inside the company. I wanted to ask them if I could meet Mr. Buffett. If they said it wasn't possible, I planned to apologize for any inconvenience and leave the company politely. Thus, I entered the company.

However, as soon as I entered Mr. Buffett's company, something unexpected happened. I was accosted by the company's receptionist.

The inside of Mr. Buffett's company was a quiet space with not many people around. I wandered around just for a moment inside. Still, I ended up catching the attention of the receptionist.

The receptionist's expression didn't seem too pleased. I had a feeling that something was amiss. I tried to leave the company right away. It seemed clear that not anyone could meet Mr. Buffett. Moreover, Mr. Buffett's company was not a place where just anyone could enter. Otherwise, the receptionist wouldn't have been uncomfortable with my presence.

However, before I could leave, the receptionist caught me.

He asked me why I had come. At first, I couldn't provide a straightforward answer to that question. It didn't feel appropriate to say that I had come to meet Mr. Buffett. He was a busy man with his own responsibilities. I couldn't simply barge in uninvited.

I tried to apologize and leave the company, feeling like I had intruded on the receptionist. But the receptionist stopped me and insisted that he needed to know why I had come.

I hesitated for a moment. No matter how I thought about it, my reason for coming to Mr. Buffett's company seemed trivial. So, I was planning to just repeat that I had come here by mistake and leave the company. However, when I saw the serious look in his eyes as he asked me the reason for my visit, I eventually opened my mouth.

"I came to meet Mr. Buffett."

The receptionist didn't seem too pleased. All I had was a feeling of apology towards both Mr. Buffett and the receptionist.

But the receptionist patiently listened to my story. I added some explanations with a sense of guilt.

"I know that it takes $4 million to have lunch with Mr. Buffett. So, originally, I didn't plan to come to meet Mr. Buffett. However, due to a misunderstanding, I came to inquire if I could meet Mr. Buffett. I'm really sorry."

I apologized to the receptionist. He remained silent.

As I began to talk about the lunch with Mr. Buffett, the receptionist's expression softened slightly. It seemed like he thought I at least knew the official way to meet Mr. Buffett. He appeared to have realized that I was aware of the fact that meeting Mr. Buffett was not an easy task.

However, he still remained silent, quietly observing me. I apologized once again to the receptionist and said I would leave.

I attempted to turn away. It didn't seem like the receptionist was trying to stop me from leaving. However, whether it was curiosity or not, the receptionist asked me a question.

"Why do you want to meet Mr. Buffett?"

I was surprised that he had asked me a question. I had thought he would just escort me out.

But I didn't know how to respond. Even I didn't know why I wanted to meet Mr. Buffett.

Still, strangely, something came to my mind. I somehow felt like I realized why I wanted to meet Mr. Buffett. Thus, I replied to him, "I know that Mr. Buffett has helped many people. My dream is to become someone like him. So, I hoped that if Mr. Buffett believes I could be like him, he would meet me."

I think all I wanted from the beginning was to become someone like Mr. Buffett, whom I admired. It was quite funny that I didn't realize the reason until the receptionist asked me why I wanted to meet him.

The receptionist began to look at me again. It was difficult to discern what he was thinking from the depths of his gaze. He then asked one last question, "What do you want me to do for you?"

I was taken aback by his question. I didn't really want him to do anything for me. I just wanted to ensure that I wouldn't cause him any stress. However, for some reason, the receptionist was asking me if I wanted something. I briefly pondered what to say.

Suddenly, I remembered the gift I had prepared for Mr. Buffett. It was none other than a letter I wrote for him. It was the letter that contained all my stories. I asked the receptionist if it would be possible to deliver the letter to Mr. Buffett. I had been carrying it with me every day in case I had the chance to meet him. The receptionist agreed to deliver the letter to Mr. Buffett. He mentioned that if Mr. Buffett liked the letter, there might be a chance for me to meet him. However, if he didn't find the letter appealing, meeting Mr. Buffett might not be possible.

I thanked the receptionist and accepted his offer to deliver the letter. A while later, I was notified that my request to meet Mr. Buffett had been declined.

After the meeting with Mr. Buffett fell through, I found myself with little to do. At the time, I was a college student. The obvious course of action was to return to my university. However, I couldn't go back to college right away because my flight back to the city where I lived was scheduled for a week later. I had tried to minimize expenses when coming to Omaha, even going as far as removing any flight schedule change options. As a result, I had no choice but to stay in Omaha until my flight.

I spent most of my time in the boarding house found through the Airbnb platform. I didn't have the funds to go out and do much. During this time, I frequently encountered the owner of the boarding house, Ryan.

I had rented a room in this boarding house for a very low price. I hadn't rented the entire house; it was just a single room. Interestingly, despite the low cost, the facilities at this place were quite good. I was essentially renting a room for the price of a hamburger combo each day, which felt incredibly cheap to me. Usually, renting a house cost a lot more.

Initially, I rarely crossed paths with Ryan because he was often busy and seldom at home. I essentially had the entire house to myself. Strangely, I couldn't help but think that I was getting an incredible deal.

Ryan was a young man who had recently left his parents' home to get married. The house where I was staying was actually a place that Ryan had just purchased. He had put it up on Airbnb until his future spouse moved in.

Airbnb recommended offering the place at a lower rate to first-time hosts like Ryan. This allowed them to confirm that the property was indeed in good condition. Offering the house at a lower price also helped build a positive reputation for hosts. It wasn't a bad deal for them either. That's why I was able to rent my room in his wonderful house at a low price.

Up until then, Ryan and I hadn't really talked much. I was also busy going to Buffett's company every day. Moreover, Ryan had a lot to prepare for his wedding. He was about to get married within a few months.

However, after the disappointment of not meeting Buffett, I started spending more time at home. I even went up to the living room, because being alone in my room all the time felt stifling.

As I spent more time in the living room, I had the chance to greet Ryan when he occasionally came home. And sometimes, when he had the time, we had quite lengthy conversations.

Ryan was really busy with wedding preparations. His future spouse even had a child. There was a lot to take care of.

One day, Ryan had an unusually dark expression on his face, which didn't suit his usual cheerful demeanor. He seemed like he needed someone to talk to, someone who would listen to his concerns. People often find comfort in sharing their troubles with others. I could sense that he had some issues he wanted to discuss. I asked him what was on his mind.

Ryan was candid and shared his recent concerns with me.

One of the issues he was dealing with involved his future stepdaughter. There had been problems arising from her mistreatment of ants. She kept hurting them. Ryan had reprimanded her, telling her not to do such things.

However, his stern approach had caused his stepdaughter to become fearful of him. She found him somewhat unfamiliar. Ryan expressed self-blame, wondering if he should have used a gentler tone when addressing the issue.

Throughout our conversation, he appeared preoccupied with self-reproach and concern for the child who would soon become his stepdaughter. I was unsure of what to say in response to his confession, as I wasn't sure how best to offer comfort or advice in that situation.

I told him honestly, "I have an older sister."

Ryan began to listen attentively to my story.

"My sister hardly ever listens to me. She didn't even let me change the channel on TV when we were watching it together. When I tried to change the channel last time, she threw a radio on me and kicked me out of our house. I couldn't get back to my house until my parents came back. Whenever I said something she didn't like, she scolded me. Sometimes, she got so angry that it seemed like she was going overboard."

My older sister was someone who scolded me every day. She even called our father once, asking if it was okay to hit me with a golf club for standing up to her. She was like a soldier. She always told me to stay strong. Sometimes, her expression was so strong that I couldn't handle it.

However, I still liked my sister. So, I explained to Ryan why I felt that way.

"But when I was going through a tough time, my sister was the one who worried about me the most. She was also the one who cried for me when I went through really bad news. That's why I like my sister so much. Maybe if you can comfort your daughter when she's having a hard time, she might come to like you too?"

I said that and fell silent. I couldn't be sure if my words provided any comfort, but Ryan didn't seem as downcast as before. I was relieved that his worries seemed to have eased somewhat. After that, whenever Ryan ran into me, he would greet me warmly. At least until he got married, I was the only person he had at his house. So, until his wedding, I was like his family.

Then one day, Ryan asked me why I had come to Omaha. I was a bit reluctant to tell him the truth. I had come to meet Mr. Buffett. However, I couldn't meet him. I had come to Omaha for an unattainable goal. It wasn't easy to share a failed experience.

Still, I wanted to be honest with Ryan. Ryan often shared his honest stories with me. I wanted to be a person who could be straightforward with him in return. Thus, I told him that I had come to Omaha to meet Mr. Buffett.

I shared all the stories about my journey, including why I wanted to meet Mr. Buffett. I thought that sharing my story of failure would make me feel sad, but surprisingly, it was quite cathartic. Failure wasn't all that bad, perhaps because meeting Mr. Buffett was a dream and a journey I had chosen for myself. It felt like I was experiencing a life I had personally chosen. I wasn't dictated by others in Omaha. I was alive.

However, for some reason, Ryan became even more serious, which made me feel awkward. I had hoped Ryan would find my stories amusing. If he enjoyed my stories, I planned to end my journey with laughter.

Ryan, who had been quietly listening to my stories, suddenly asked me a question. He said, "So, do you really want to meet Mr. Buffett?" His serious tone caught me off guard, but I decided to be honest with him.

"Yes, I do," I replied.

Ryan simply said, "Okay," and then asked me to wait for a moment. I was puzzled by what he was up to. He took out his phone and made a call. Soon, he began speaking on the phone.

"Mom!" he exclaimed.

He moved a bit away from me to continue the call. I couldn't hear what he was saying. However, I could see the bright expression on his face throughout the call. Ryan really loved his parents. I thought he would make a good parent himself. Someone who loves their parents would likely become a good parent too.

Soon, the call ended. Ryan began speaking with excitement in his voice.

"Mr. Buffett holds an annual shareholders' meeting," he said.

I didn't understand what he meant. I didn't even know what a shareholders' meeting was. However, Ryan's tone and mood were very unusual. He seemed like something joyous had just happened to him.

"Most CEOs don't attend shareholder meetings, but Mr. Buffett is different. He attends the annual shareholders' meeting every year."

I felt a shiver run down my spine as if a cold winter wind had brushed against my skin. It felt like an unbelievable coincidence was waiting for me.

"However, my mom owns some shares of Buffett's company. They're not that significant, just affordable for anyone. But thanks to that, my mother has tickets to attend the shareholder meeting where Mr. Buffett is present," Ryan explained. He pointed to his phone and continued, "I just asked my mom if she could give you one of those tickets, and she said she could."

Ryan took a deep breath and then asked me, "Do you still want to meet Mr. Buffett?"

I was momentarily speechless, unsure of what to say. It felt as if I were the only one frozen in time, unable to move forward.

The entire story seemed to be passing through me once again, with memories from the past flooding back.

At first, I thought I came to Omaha because I wanted to meet Mr. Buffett. Maybe I was wrong. I guess I came to Omaha to meet myself.

Made in United States
Troutdale, OR
01/02/2025

27492710R00106